RECLAIM YOUR SPIRITUAL NATURE

walk within

An Advent, Solstice, & Christmas Path

CRYSTAL L. STEINBERG

More Books by Crystal Steinberg

*Walk Within: Reclaim Your Spiritual Nature—
A Companion Journal*

*Turning Point: Empowering Stories to Activate the
Divine Feminine Within*

 FLOWER *of* LIFE PRESS

Walk Within—Reclaim Your Spiritual Nature: An Advent, Solstice, & Christmas Path

Copyright © 2022 Crystal L. Steinberg

All rights reserved. No part of this publication may be reproduced, distributed, or transmitted in any form or by any means, including photocopying, recording, or other electronic or mechanical methods, without the prior written permission of the publisher, except in the case of brief quotations embodied in critical reviews and certain other noncommercial uses permitted by copyright law.

Disclaimer
The ideas and suggestions contained within *Walk Within* are not intended to diagnose, treat, prevent, or cure any disease or condition and are intended for informational purposes only. Each person's physical, emotional, and spiritual condition is unique. The information in this book is not a substitute for medical or psychological treatment from licensed and registered healthcare professionals. You should seek professional medical advice before making any health decision. Neither the author nor the publisher shall be liable or responsible for any damage allegedly arising from the practices in this book.

Published by Flower of Life Press
Hadlyme, CT, USA
Astara J. Ashley, *Publisher*
www.floweroflifepress.com

Cover and interior design by Astara Jane Ashley, floweroflifepress.com
Cover Art by Crystal L. Steinberg

Library of Congress Control Number: Available Upon Request

ISBN-13: 979-8-9864729-6-6

Printed in the United States of America

Praise

"I read pretty fast, but not this book. It contains people and ideas I have not yet encountered. This work took me on an unexplored journey. Serious readers will not return to their previous lives. They will see with new eyes, minds, and spirits and be born anew."

—*Elizabeth Scmidt-Kuhr, BS, MSE, and CEAP.*

"Unlearning Religion is a key concept for human liberation. Religion has been an integral part of the patriarchal coercion that has demeaned women, exploited nature, and limited sexual and gender freedom. Dr. Steinberg offers a new vision of what religion can be when infused with the sacred feminine and masculine, a deep alignment with nature, and a celebration of race, gender, and sexual freedom."

—*Jim Garrison, Founder and President of Ubiquity University and Convenor of Humanity Rising*

"Crystal has an amazing gift for asking thought-provoking questions. Pre-reading reflection questions invite us to look at where we are with our knowledge base and beliefs. Crystal then shares research, personal stories, and biblical interpretations to expand and enrich what we know. Post-reading integration questions offer us the opportunity to walk within. We can discover the many possible answers that can change our agreements and beliefs creating a more loving story. Using this book in community adds support and richness to our journey. Thank you, Crystal for sharing your gifts and message."

—*Robin Dahl, High School Mathematics Educator and Client*

Dedication

For Matthew and Charleigh,

our beautiful grandchildren.

Thank you for never letting us forget

where we come from and

the Beauty of every moment

on the Earth.

Your Tears and Laughter

Yield Ears to Hear and

Your Joy and Sorrows

Give Us Eyes to See

the Gifts of Light and Darkness.

NOT Anthropos Andros

Contents

Introduction 1

Chapter 1
Colonization of Land, Hearts, and Minds 7

Chapter 2
Reclaiming Divine Feminine and Sacred Masculine Energies 27

Chapter 3
Where Do Bibles Come From? 49

Chapter 4
The Revised Common Lectionary Passages for the Journey 65

Chapter 5
What is Coming? Advent Week I: Year A 77

Chapter 6
What If There Is No Sin? Advent Week II: Year A 101

Chapter 7
Orthodoxy and Heresy–Advent Week III: Year A 125

Chapter 8
Preparing the Way For Mary–Advent Week IV: Year A 153

Chapter 9
Womb Awakening–Solstice/Christmas: Year A 177

Chapter 10
Initiation–First Sunday After Solstice/Christmas: Year A 199

Conclusion 222
Acknowledgments 228
Endnotes 230
Bibliography 232
About the Author 235

Introduction

The times in which we live demand our awareness. Code red climate change and the weather conditions it brings, world pandemics and their viral mutations, and emerging autocratic leaders compromising democratic ideals can be so overwhelming that it feels like the world is ending. Community collapse and the changes it brings require us to search for meaning within ourselves. Deep within each of us is the mystery of wounds with corresponding gifts we may use to heal them. If we don't see these aspects in ourselves, we won't be able to find them in the world. Nor will we be able to help sustain, heal, and renew it. In the context of galaxies and the cosmos we may appear insignificant, but on earth, we co-create with all sentient beings in the light and shadow of consciousness.

When I took the time provided by covid isolation to look within myself, I discovered a core wound of abandonment. As I examined this abandonment in the context of Religious Trauma Syndrome becoming more and more prevalent these days, I realized I held agreements, some conscious and some subconscious, about God, religion, and the church. I also realized the spiritual bypass often required to make and hold the agreements. Consequently, this book employs aspects of my journey within, the realized agreements surrounding Spirit, and an exploration of the variables informing them. Each of us makes our own agreements according to stories that we have subconsciously inherited, that we tell ourselves, or that others tell us. Often, curiosities fostered by our life experiences prompt us to examine these agreements.

For instance, in this life, I arrived in a Christian family with a blue-collar work ethic. As a creative life-long learner, I volunteered at church for decades, graduated from undergraduate school with a

Bachelor of Arts (BA) in Philosophy and English, obtained a Master of Arts in Teaching (MAT) degree, taught in a Jesuit High School where I founded and coordinated an academic support program, and consulted at The Art Institute of Chicago. A decade later, I attended seminary, obtained a Master of Divinity (MDiv) degree, was ordained, and served as a Lutheran parish pastor and mission developer. Many of these things count as expertise according to the culture in which we live.

When my mother became terminally ill, I went on leave from call to serve as her primary caregiver. What I personally experienced during this time challenged everything that I thought I knew. It helped me realize how the universe had been communicating with me in the past, and how I didn't have ears to hear nor eyes to see it. The more aware I became, the more the universe spoke to me in a variety of ways.

An interspecies relationship developed and grew between plants, trees, and myself after I became an Aromatherapist in the Magdalene (Myrrhophore) tradition. Invitations to tribal ceremonies through the years expanded my awareness. Shamanic journeys introduced and enhanced my relationship with animals, ancestors, and spirit guides, and I became aware of every sentient being sharing consciousness.

My heart deeply resonates with Toltec Wisdom, and I continue to deepen my awareness and practice in its tradition through my teacher, HeatherAsh Amara, the author of *Warrior Goddess Training*. The Warrior Goddess Training Circles that she facilitates include teachings and small group sharing that also inform my agreements.

The information used in my contemplations can supplement walks within from a variety of perspectives. If you live in the United States and wonder how we arrived at where we are today, a walk within can offer information to help untangle the chaos. If you are a non-Christian American citizen and are curious about the influence Christianity has on your life, the walk can be illuminating. If you were or are a Christian feeling restless, sensing different ways of knowing or identifying mystical experiences in your life, this journey can serve as a bridge, or a reinforcement of a bridge, to a new way of living.

If you are interested in growing beyond a religious understanding of Jesus and Mary Magdalene to a more personal understanding of them, this book provides a safe space to explore. If you have heard about lost gospels and are curious about what wasn't included in the bible, the journey contains passages from the Gnostic Gospel of Mary for consideration. Four canonical gospels provide a limited variety of perspectives. Adding the perspective of a previously excluded gospel helps readers experience a dynamic, rather than static, wisdom tradition offered by ancient writings. As we actively engage with them, we co-create new possibilities and meaning for the future.

While I share some of my own familial, educational, occupational, religious, and civic experiences, the agreements that I make accordingly are illustrations and not prescriptions. The foundation of this book is built on the idea that each one of us travels our own path. Experience and impact are not necessarily related when we think about cause and effect. They often combine with other experiences and realizations to expand consciousness. Different points of view can stimulate growth and change in us anywhere along the way.

In the journey of writing this book, I continue reviewing my own agreements developed as a child, a wife, a nurturing mother and grandmother, a midwife helping birth the lives of students, parishioners, and clients, an educator, a parish pastor, a caregiver, a wounded healer, and a wisdom keeper. Through the Toltec practice of recapitulation, I explore how I came to hold these agreements and consciously choose which to retain, which to release, what energy to reclaim, where to direct this energy and what to co-create anew. While this journey is an ongoing soul engaging process, writing a book to share it requires some semblance of format and structure. How could I examine my religious agreements about Christianity without reviewing the bible, church history, and church traditions? One of my agreements about examining the bible is to avoid proof texting—looking through the bible to find something to support my point of view regardless of its context. I ultimately decided to employ the readings from *The Revised Common Lectionary*. In short, these are the passages read in most Christian church services. It makes sense to employ these passages. They are likely the most known and influential stories whether or not someone is a Christian given Christianity's extreme impact on the western colonized world.

I narrowed the field to Sunday church readings according to seasons in the Church Year which are based on Earth seasons. The new Church Year begins with Advent and Christmas which contain the Winter Solstice and the renewal of light. These readings rotate once every three years according to the schedule of Matthew: Year A, Mark: Year B, and Luke: Year C, with readings from John integrated monthly. November 27, 2022, begins church Year A with passages primarily from the Gospel of Matthew. Year A begins again in 2025, then 2028, and so on.

This book is the first in an Unlearning Religious Dogma Series reframing these assigned Sunday bible readings in the context of a non-canonical gospel. It offers you opportunities to consciously walk within and review your perspectives of Christianity and your personal experiences of God/Creator/Beloved/Source/Spirit/Wholeness/Mystery/Energy/(Other) _____. Most importantly, this journey invites you to review the agreements that inform your choices. How did you arrive at them? Do they still serve you? What energy do you employ to sustain them? Where else might you direct that energy? Are there agreements that might serve you better instead? We are always at a point of choice regarding our lives when we desire to take responsibility for them.

The first four chapters contain an exploration of variables to consider regarding the foundation and framework of this journey. The final six chapters reframe the bible readings for the beginning of the church year. This includes the Advent, Solstice, Christmas seasons. Reflection prompts prior to each chapter, and integration prompts following each one, provide space for journaling, drawing, doodling, collaging, or whatever works best for your responses.

The *Walk Within: Reclaim Your Spiritual Nature—A Companion Journal* provides space for any overflow. In this manner, the book seeks to help facilitate, rather than direct your path. Neuroscience suggests that the physical act of creating in any way can help rewire the brain through the central nervous system. This is an especially powerful tool as we seek to review and generate agreements for thriving in today's quickly changing world.

Enjoy hospitality and community along the journey through weekly virtual zoom gatherings. Visit **crystalsteinbergcocreating.com** for more information.

CHAPTER 1

Colonization of Land, Hearts, and Minds

PRE-READING REFLECTIONS

1. Without doing any research, based on the information that you have at this moment, how would you describe your indigenous roots?

2. What do you know about the Indigenous people of North America? How did you learn these things?

3. Describe, depict, or collage your relationship with the Earth:

4. Some people describe themselves as "spiritual" rather than "religious." How do you understand this distinction?

THE NEED TO RECLAIM ENERGY

We often inherit what our culture calls beliefs from our families, absorb them from our culture or create them by filling in the gaps of missing information as we tell stories. Embedded in these beliefs are agreements we have made most often unconsciously. Influences such as a Puritan Ethic, questions regarding Indigeneity, a lack of separation between Church and State, Religious Trauma Syndrome, Spiritual Bypass, and Newtonian Physics contribute to the colonization of the land, our hearts, and our minds which separates us from our spiritual nature. When this happens, beliefs replace personal knowing through resonance. We give our energy away whenever we ignore resonance and don't consciously make agreements.

Reclaiming our Spiritual Nature helps us identify and develop the spiritual gifts that connect us with our personal knowing through resonance. This helps us review and consciously make agreements that enable us to reclaim the energy required to sustain them or prompts us to release them. Recognizing and processing how we give away our energy through these agreements enables us to reclaim the energy and direct it for other purposes.

INFLUENCES OF PURITAN ETHIC

"How many of you were born here in the United States?" the facilitator of our virtual Ancestral Healing class asked. Most of us raised our hands. "How many of your parents were born here?" Nearly the same majority of the 100 participants raised our hands. "Grandparents?" While a visibly smaller group, most of us still raised our hands. But when she asked about our great-grandparents, none of us raised our hands. A clear delineation regarding immigration appeared before our eyes.

Hundreds of years ago, immigrants left their relationships with their literal homelands to travel to a new land where the government practiced genocide against the indigenous people found there. As a result, people started living compromised relationships with the land

and the energy that the Earth provides. This happened in a variety of ways: slavery, loss of lineage when leaving the indigenous rituals and ceremonies previously practiced, fear of practicing them in a new place where one may be persecuted for it, ignorance of the rituals and ceremonies practiced by indigenous peoples of the Americas, and a judgmental Puritan Ethic such as that described in Nathaniel Hawthorne's *The Scarlet Letter* or Arthur Miller's *The Crucible*.

This Puritan Ethic stems from a Judeo-Christian tradition containing a theology of dominion over the Earth and a fundamental theology of right and wrong. Accordingly, choices and actions became viewed as either right or wrong in and of themselves rather than part of living in harmony with the Earth and a variety of perspectives. This ethic gave way to religious ritual and ceremony celebrating one "God" in one "right" way as opposed to the indigenous rituals and ceremonies celebrating spiritual energetic presences in all that exists. Consequently, the "right" ways were embedded in our institutions and systems of organization.

Distance grew between us and our spiritual gifts such as Automatic Writing, Clairaudience, Claircognizance, Clairsentience, Clairsentinence, Clairvoyance, Incorporation, Irradiation, and Xenoglossia. As Church and government officials convinced people that they held the authority and that people should come to them for decisions and regulations about their lives, use of gifts atrophied and vanished. At the same time, voids expanded between Hearts and Minds, between humans, between humans and the Earth (the elements of air, earth, fire, and water), between humans and animals, birds, plants, trees, stones, mountains, minerals, stars, planets, galaxies, and the mystery of the unknown.

This lack of connection culminates today in events such as current code red climate change, global pandemics, and the threat of nuclear war in Ukraine. Specifically in the United States, it has led to weekly mass shootings that slaughter innocents and the repeal of Roe v. Wade. This repeal was made by a compromised Supreme Court and politicians such as Rep. Lauren Boebert (R-CO) saying that they are tired of separation of church and state in the U.S. Boebert added that she believes 'the church is supposed to direct the government.'"[1] We have either reached the limits of the rational mind or denied its limitations all along. No logical response, alone, can overcome the challenges of this unsustainable way to live. Mindfully acknowledging the nation's history and processing our agreements that enabled it to reach this point give us energy to generate new agreements that foster a more sustainable way to live.

INDIGENEITY

Cultural appropriation occurs when we adopt something as if it is our own without invitation, education, experience, or initiation. The lack of these experiences leads to misappropriation. Although we all have indigenous roots, most Americans did not maintain their lineages of the stories, rituals, and ceremonies honoring the Earth as we grew and developed. Some people research ancestry for answers only to face roadblocks when the leads cease. Others turn to DNA testing for answers, but test results do not equal a lifetime of wisdom learning, ritual, and ceremonial practice. With gratitude, we acknowledge the many indigenous tribes inviting, sharing, and helping to lead us back to inner knowing and a spiritual relationship with the Earth. Resources such as The Heart Math Institute teach and collect data around building heart coherence with the frequency of the Earth. Fortunately, we can reclaim energy and fuel our intentions with it.

CHRISTIAN INFLUENCE ON AMERICAN INSTITUTIONS

Despite living in a nation supposedly upholding the separation of church and state, our governments and institutions are organized around a Judeo-Christian ethic. Whether or not we are practicing Christians, many of our beliefs and agreements stem subconsciously from Christian influence on American culture. Consider the number of biblical allusions found in required school reading and the cultural calendar—federal holidays organized by events in Christianity as well as the atrocities supported by Christianity. Presidents place their hands on one ancient wisdom text, The Bible, during the inauguration, rather than on a stack of texts acknowledging the variety of beliefs within the country. Who wants to be on the marginalized side of a religion used to support slavery, genocide, and inquisitions?

One of the ways to help reclaim spiritual energy allocated to religion is to recapitulate canonized interpretation of scripture. Church leaders met in councils to determine the canon and ordered all other texts destroyed. The discovery of these "lost" texts during our lifetimes invites consideration of them in and of themselves, in the context of other texts, and in terms of our lives. Such ongoing contemplation keeps our understanding open and fluid rather than static and inflexible. It allows us to continue learning and developing connections rather than separations.

RELIGIOUS TRAUMA SYNDROME

"Religious Trauma Syndrome" is becoming an ever-increasing diagnosis these days. The Christian dogma of original sin, something that believers can't do anything about like the color of their eyes and the threat of eternal damnation prompt believers to look outside of themselves for a savior. This disconnects them from their spiritual natures, from the divine within themselves and from responsibility for their lives. Numbing replaces thriving through various addictions and behaviors such as self-righteousness, judgment and "might as right." Crusades, Inquisitions, Slavery and Genocide in the name of God demonstrate the results of such wounded fragmentation.

Even when the internal conflict between dogma and spiritual nature becomes too much and believers leave religion, the wounding often continues rather than heals. Losses of community, a sense of belonging and purpose cause wandering without a clear sense of direction. When I left the church roster, I decided like Huck Finn while tearing up his letter reporting the runaway slave Jim, "to go to hell then." But even this decision remained within the dogma of the church.

Recapitulating agreements about hell and making conscious choices about its existence help heal wounds. Without conscious practice, leaving the church does not necessarily mean that the dogma leaves the person. Low self-esteem, lack of trust and indecision are wounds that can take lifetimes to heal.

In the words of Kurt Vonnegut in *Slaughterhouse Five*, "So it goes." Slowly but surely, we can give our energy away to religion, becoming less and less aware of the Wisdom within us, until we are left waiting. Waiting for someone to come and rescue us rather than taking responsibility for our lives and identifying teachers with wisdom to share with us. Wisdom that helps equip us to do our own work, to grow our consciousness, to live authentically, to die to our guilt and shame, and to ascend to an expanded awareness each day. Such awareness recognizes the interconnectedness of all that exists. It helps foster empathy, compassion, and love.

SPIRITUAL BYPASS

Spiritual Bypass is one of the ways we can avoid such work. Personal or institutional issues that we ignore, hoping they will disappear, fall into this category. Rather than working through difficult emotions or confronting unresolved issues, people and leaders simply dismiss them with spiritual explanations. Phrases such as "God has a plan" and "In God we Trust" can become toxic dismissals of our responsibility. These words can grow into strategies to protect ourselves or to maintain peace by suppressing feelings rather than resolving issues.

Spirituality can be a force that helps enhance an individual's, a community's, or the world's well-being. But engaging in spiritual bypassing to avoid complicated feelings or issues can ultimately stifle growth. Spirituality, too, has a shadow side, but we tend to idealize it. When we know that someone (most importantly ourselves) or something (such as institutions) have become toxic, we need to clear the air and cleanse. Feelings need to be processed, harmful actions require apologies **and** changes to restore justice, balance, and harmony. We must acknowledge our responsibility as co-creators of the world in which we live rather than waiting for someone to save us from ourselves.

As I am revising this book, Pope Francis is in Canada on what he calls a "penitential pilgrimage." He is apologizing to First Nations for the atrocities experienced at the hands of catholic priests, nuns, and workers in residential schools. More than 150,000 Native children in Canada were taken from their homes from the 19th century until the 1970s and placed in these schools to separate them from their culture. Recently the remains of 10,000 children who died under the supervision of these "brothers and sisters" were discovered. Most died at the hands of these workers. A review of the press coverage of his tour shows the Pope's language becoming stronger and stronger until he refers to the events that occurred in the church-run residential schools as "genocide."

Yet, by design, the church as an institution refuses to take responsibility for such atrocities. Instead, they project harm done onto individual "brothers and sisters" and assume no responsibility for church teachings and leadership. This is the same for other institutions and corporations. We live in a time when we struggle with holding communities accountable for their teachings and actions while at the same time providing space for imperfection and restorative justice. For instance, embedded deep within the Canadian residential schools' atrocities is an agreement about the church as an institution remaining sinless. If it admits its imperfections, how does it maintain authority and power? Notice the pronoun we use to reference institutions. American culture objectifies "it" as inanimate, something without feeling, responsibility, or accountability. Giving away our power and responsibility enables institutions to use them to avoid accountability.

Questions emerge about institutional spiritual bypass in such circumstances. Are prayers begging for forgiveness nothing more than Spiritual Bypass without accountability? Do we practice spiritual bypass ourselves when we do not hold church leaders accountable for the institutions they lead? What agreements do we make when we say institutions are not responsible for their actions? How do we hold ourselves accountable for our own actions without judgment and shame? Experience and research reveal many types of bypassing. Find the most prevalent charted below for further consideration.

Bypass	Qualities	Ways to Reduce Bypassing
Aggrandizement	Seeking to be more enlightened, superior, or more awakened than others. Claiming to reach spiritual milestones can mask perceived deficiencies and insecurities.	Cultivate an Open Mind; willing to be wrong, misguided, or totally off the mark. Listening to doubt is intelligent.
Finger-Pointing	Getting caught up in what is wrong with others, even our teachers and guides, and instilling a false sense of self-righteousness. Replacing the need to look inside and to work on ourselves.	Practice open mindedness by asking questions from different perspectives: What am I not seeing? Is this hurting me in some way? Is this harming others in any way?
Guru	Treating the words of gurus, shamans, and spiritual teachers as irrefutable truth and failing to think for ourselves. Forgetting the purpose of listening to their wisdom and integrating the essence of their teachings into our unique lives.	Evaluate teachings through examination, application, experiences, and integration.

Bypass	Qualities	Ways to Reduce Bypassing
Optimist	Only focusing on the positive and only seeing the glass half full. Can be an indication of the inability to deal with negative emotions.	Examine the light and shadow side of actions. Consider hypothetical possibilities: What is the other side of this? What could go wrong? How has this hurt someone in the past?
Prayer	When circumventing personal responsibility by putting faith in a higher being (typically granting authority to an institution or person set aside for this purpose) thereby making us passive rather than trusting ourselves to act when necessary.	Assess whether prayers are an escape from or a means to face pain.
Psychonaut	Using psychedelics to escape daily life and to avoid the work of personal development.	Seek a variety of perspectives. Monitor use with a trained professional.
Readings	Looking outside ourselves for guidance (such as readings and horoscopes) because we are afraid of taking responsibility for our lives in the unknown and/or because we do not trust ourselves.	Study the tools of the type of reading used for guidance. Research, experience, and observe the impact of variables to compare with readings.

Bypass	Qualities	Ways to Reduce Bypassing
Saint	Thinking that promotes the underlying belief that spiritual people can't have shadow sides because that makes them "unspiritual." Often accompanied by martyr complexes.	Face Cognitive Dissonance: Where are my agreements and actions out of alignment?
Spirit Guide	While at times it is helpful to feel the support and help of spirit guides, it becomes a problem when they become crutches. Relying on them fully, without any of our own insights, inhibits the growth of spiritual character.	Note affirmations or detractions occurring while interacting with guides. Journal experiences for ongoing discernment.
Victim	Being a victim of one's gifts, taking away the pressure of co-creating one's life and happiness.	Ask the questions: How is this making me weak or dependent? Is this hurting me in some way?

Spiritual awareness requires a great deal of energy in today's dynamic context of constant change. Things can't be set in stone as we mistakenly expected from previous science and religion. Our awareness is in direct proportion to the amount of energy we retain and distribute by conscious agreement. Becoming aware of our agreements, reviewing them, and determining by what agreements we desire to live is now necessary for survival. This work can no longer be considered a luxury of a wealthy, thriving lifestyle.

NEWTONIAN PHYSICS SHIFTING TO QUANTUM PHYSICS

Recent Quantum Physics discoveries provide paradigm shifts affirming the potential of Intuitive, Imaginative, and Creative Intelligences to help address change. They document that everything is composed of particles and waves that move and create energy. These are measured in frequency. Energy connects everything. This begs the question: Are we humans who experience spirit, spirits experiencing what it means to be human, or both? The culture of the United States previously answered this question as humans who experience spirit. Connected to this response are the three ideas of Newtonian physics that permeate western culture: observe, predict, and control. Newton's physics derived from his theology that supported his scientific research. In this context, spiritual matters, often disparaged as "New Age," were marginalized and considered "woo-woo."

Quantum physics now gives spirituality a context that can no longer be marginalized due to a lack of scientific evidence. The divine within, including spiritual gifts such as Automatic Writing, Clairaudience, Claircognizance, Clairsentience, Clairsentinence, Clairvoyance, Incorporation, Irradiation, and Xenoglossia, are ours to claim, develop, and manage as we cross the threshold into the mystery of co-creation. While transitioning toward this threshold, many experience the future pull of the Earth, but we won't know how to respond without awareness of our indigenous roots and the gifts they carry.

POST-READING INTEGRATIONS

1. Which of the variables explored in this chapter most informs your agreements about God/Creator/Beloved/Source/Spirit/Wholeness/Mystery/Energy/(Other) _____? How?

2. Go to the following link to learn more about HeartMath and to enjoy a free experience: **heartmath.org/training/heart-math-experience.** Then describe your experience and what you learned:

Colonization of Land, Hearts, and Minds

3. What kind of practices yield similar results for you?

4. How would you direct energy gathered through such practices?

CHAPTER 2

Reclaiming Divine Feminine and Sacred Masculine Energies

PRE-READING REFLECTIONS

1. What are your understandings of "patriarchy" and "misogyny?"

2. What does Divine Feminine energy look like, and how does it work within you?

3. What does Sacred Masculine energy look like, and how does it work within you?

NO VENERATION OF WOMEN

When I was a Lutheran teaching in a Jesuit high school, I felt uncomfortable when the day started with a "Hail Mary." Lutherans theologically don't venerate women. They tell the story of the virgin birth through the creeds they pray, inherited from the councils generating the biblical canon, but they do not pray to any women. I didn't want to model *not* praying for my students, but I also did not desire to inauthentically pray. One day this conflict bothered me so deeply that I went to the vice principal who offered the morning prayers to request that he no longer pray the "Hail Mary" to open the school day. I explained that it put non-catholics in a difficult position. After listening patiently, he said, "Thanks for your input" and prayed the "Hail Mary" again the next morning.

I don't know if it was out of conviction for being a catholic institution, a belief in the veneration of women, or just a "this is the way we do things here" that led to the next day's prayer. It is ironic that the catholic religion doesn't allow women to preach and to serve as pastors, yet it venerates women, while the Lutheran institution does not venerate women, yet it ordains women to preach and to serve as pastors. This irony surfaces another conflict. All of Christianity systematically subjugates women in one way or another. Such subjugation and objectification led to the destruction and eventual disappearance of the Divine Feminine and the Sacred Masculine.

DIVINE FEMININE AND SACRED MASCULINE ENERGIES

Throughout history, human personification of the divine involved integrated male and female energies in a variety of ways. The God of ancient Israel was understood by its earliest worshippers to be "dual-gendered." Israelite priests would have read the four Hebrew letters of God's name, YHWH, in reverse, pronouncing the name Hu/Hi, Hebrew for "He/She." Earliest reports also show the energies integrated by Indigenous Peoples. Native Americans reference "The One who Created the Earth" without a male or female distinction. Other Indigenous people around the world integrate the energies through masculine and feminine consorts: Celtic/Druid (Dagda and Danu) West African (Amma and Oshun), Egyptian (Isis and Osiris), Native American (Mother Earth and Father Sky), Hebrew (Yahweh and Asherah), Toltec (Quetzalcoatl and Tezcatlipoca), and Christian (Jesus and Mother Mary). Today, reviews of ancient Wisdom texts reveal Jesus and Mary Magdalene stepping forward to challenge the patriarchal dominance within Christianity and its authority in the western world.

The history of the Divine Feminine is not the focus of this Advent, Solstice, Christmas journey but understanding the significance of the eventual exclusion of the Divine Feminine and the exclusion's impact is. Challenges to the Divine Feminine arose when masculine and feminine energies were linked to gender. Personifying god as only male led to the objectification of women. This objectification birthed the Madonna/whore syndrome. Women became either objects left untouched on pedestals or dirty whores/witches requiring destruction due to their association with the material world. Associating the female gender with the earth enabled the objectification of the earth as well. Objectification bred a transactional relationship between humans and the earth as humans claimed dominion over the earth rather than seeking a relationship of mutual respect. This lack of mutual respect contributes to the code red climate change situation that we navigate today.

Subjugation and objectification disconnect both men and women from their Divine Feminine and Sacred Masculine energies. Disconnection from these energies places the energies outside of ourselves rather than within us. This leaves us denying energy rather than accessing it. The opening story of this chapter demonstrates my inability to venerate Mary given agreements fostered by my religious affiliation. During the Reformation, Mary, the mother of Jesus, was lost with much of the art depicting her when reformers destroyed anything considered "catholic." Despite desiring to only reform the church with his 95 theses, politicians and other followers of Martin Luther sought a way to separate and create a different church. Martin Luther never intended this. Original ideas often disappear in the application process. Discoveries of ancient texts also demonstrate this as they continue to challenge the applications of Jesus' teachings since their inception.

PRICE OF DISCONNECTION

Disconnection also causes us to dismiss transmissions from the universe. One of our family's favorite activities involves spending free time in bookstores, gathering a stack of books, and leafing through the pages to find a treasure to purchase. While in seminary, I attended a conference with my husband in San Diego, CA where I spent a day in the Crow's Nest, one of our nation's first independent bookstores. I purchased *The Dance of the Dissident Daughter* by Sue Monk Kidd. When I returned to the hotel, I started reading the book. That evening, I dreamt about the next chapter of the book. What I described as "a pulsating head of leaves" appeared to me. After I read the chapter about Sophia, I told my husband about how I had just dreamed something similar the previous night.

I started showing him where I stopped reading the book before retiring for the evening and shared my dreams each morning. A consistent pattern emerged. I dreamt the book as I read it! The divine feminine spoke to me and her voice impacted my preaching. This did not please my Homiletics professor who tore me to shreds in front of the entire class when I preached the story of Jesus calming the storm as a labor and delivery experience. My Divine Feminine-inspired sermon did not fit the patriarchal box.

Standing there, turning beet red, and determined not to let him see me cry, I breathed deeply as my classmates shared their silent empathy by hanging their heads. Promising myself that I could preach as inspired when I served in a parish, I misplaced the book and no longer attempted to share my Divine Feminine-inspired sermons in class. Generations practiced this type of denial, thereby maintaining the patriarchy.

FINDING OUR OWN WISDOM TEACHERS

The last Marquette University warrior mascot introduced me to Native American teachings in a required teaching certification class. I deeply resonated with what I learned, and we became friends. His wife welcomed me to her tribe's circle of women, and they invited me to participate in some of their ceremonies. As I moved and traveled, I frequently found myself in conversation with Indigenous Peoples and received invitations for further learning in tribes across the country.

The more I learned, the more I longed to find my Indigenous roots. I vaguely remembered my mom describing a secret Native connection on my father's side of the family, but he died very young and no one else acknowledged it. At this point, I narrowly defined indigeneity to only Native American tribal affiliation. Research tracing my father's lineage from England to Canada showed a possible connection to an Indian Residence School there. As I prepared to request records, I learned that a recent fire destroyed them. I heard the universe suggest that indigeneity is not tied to a bloodline, but to practices and a way of living.

When I saw a Toltec Wisdom class offered by HeatherAsh Amara at the university where I am studying for a PhD in Wisdom Studies, I remembered previously reading Don Miguel Ruiz's, *The Four Agreements*. It turned out that Amara studied with Ruiz for a decade before he challenged a group of students including her to make the teachings their own and to share them with the world. As a result, Amara's Warrior Goddess Training Circles evolved. These circles support women as they reclaim energy given away and depleted by themselves and patriarchal practices. Thankfully, The Divine Feminine has been re-emerging in a variety of ways such as this.

TOLTEC PRACTICE OF RECAPITULATION

Understanding Toltec Wisdom as a way of living rather than a religion requiring a particular set of beliefs to remain part of the community, I joined Amara's Training Circles to learn more while working toward my degree. The work suggests that we ultimately heal ourselves by taking responsibility for our lives. Accountability is part of taking responsibility for our lives—a critical aspect of Toltec Wisdom. This is not responsibility in terms of control. Nor is it responsibility seeking perfection. Rather, Toltec Responsibility acknowledges a "Dream of Reality"—cultural agreements accepted as universal givens supporting the status quo rather than agreements made consciously by individuals. Each unique being holds a perspective in consciousness.

Ironically, we often "project" our own work onto others' lives, believing that our individual views of reality are universal givens. We then use our individual views to judge or to project our woundedness on others' lives. Addressing this cycle involves raising our subconscious agreements to a conscious level and reviewing them. Eliminating energy-draining rather than life-giving agreements fosters greater connection within ourselves, the divine within and without, and the various communities with which we interact.

I agree that we, ourselves, ultimately direct and manage our healing. This requires information that we may find in practices such as recapitulation, undoing and unlearning just as we gather information about our bodies from bloodwork. I quickly benefited from the practice of recapitulation. This practice of reclaiming energy and applying it in my life intrigued me. I felt more energetic and experienced a reduction in knee pain. The way we direct our energy ultimately helps heal our wounds, helps expand our consciousness, and helps us to serve as co-creators. The more each one of us does this kind of work, the more we become accessible to creative power and may contribute to the collective consciousness' healing and expansion.

WARRIOR HEART PRACTICE

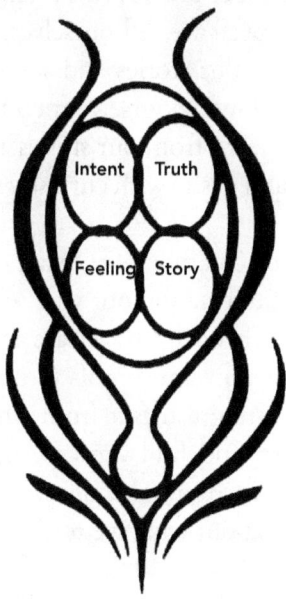

Illustrated by Kevin Flores

The most valuable practice I experienced in Amara's work involves recapitulation with a map similar to the four chambers of the human heart. She describes the process in her book by the same name, *Warrior Heart Practice*. I am summarizing it and sharing an example of using it here. Try it and if you resonate with the process, consider developing it as a practice. If not, identify practices that do help you reclaim energy and connect with personal knowing.

The work contained within the process begins in the Feeling chamber. Instead of denying or suppressing feelings, time spent in this chamber acknowledges, names, and experiences them. I find the key to remaining open while experiencing discomfort is breathwork. A four-count inhalation, a four-count hold, and a four-count exhalation calms me. Use whatever breathing pattern enables you to stay present. This allows us to be curious about our feelings rather than judging them. Once we fully acknowledge and experience our feelings, we move to the Story Chamber.

Rather than constantly retelling stories as a means of rationalization or projection, the story chamber provides a container in which to release our stories. We observe what we tell ourselves, the language we use, which agreements inform our stories and seek to listen even deeper than we previously have. Giving ourselves permission to be imperfect helps us remain open to learn from our stories as we witness the roots of any self-deprecation and desire with curiosity rather than judgment.

As we move to the Truth Chamber, we listen for what is true in the moment. We listen for information our wise self already knows, even from previous lifetimes. This helps us release agreements about being right or wrong, or about universal proofs to understand what is true for this moment? We distinguish fact from what we desire, identify the truth within context, and find ways to support ourselves being with the truth that we discover. This allows us to enter the Intent Chamber seeking clarity about what we really want in each situation.

Our intent is our focus and commitment. Without intent, we easily submit to outdated agreements, judgments, and outside forces. Intent motivates us to ask, what do I *really* want? What do I desire? What is my purpose and how does this experience connect with it? What is my focus and what word or phrase reminds me of it?

With our word or phrase of intent in mind, we re-enter the Truth Chamber with a new focus. Carrying both intent and truth as we re-enter the Story Chamber, we align our story with our consciously created intention and truth rather than a story defining our truth and intention. Freed from subconscious agreements and outside judgments, our creativity flows as we witness our new relationship to the story(ies). Consequently, as we return to the Feeling Chamber, we find ourselves more able to experience our feelings without being paralyzed by them or even discover new ones supporting the vision we have consciously chosen for our lives.

Moving through the chambers and circling back is not a one-time event. Committing to this practice strengthens abilities to identify when we become vulnerable to outdated agreements or outside influences to live according to our intents. It is difficult to describe in mere words just how this works, but the following example helps clarify it. In considering this illustration, please note that the stories shared are not told as rationalizations for my choices or as judgments of choices made by others. They provide context for the illustration.

ILLUSTRATING THE WARRIOR HEART PRACTICE

Recall the story that I shared about the Divine Feminine-inspired sermon and the responses of the Homiletics professor and my classmates. Remembering it stirs a variety of thoughts and emotions. I am recapitulating the event to illustrate the Warrior Heart Practice.

Entering the Feeling Chamber: I feel embarrassed, stupid, and abandoned.

Entering the Story Chamber: I suggest that I should have known better than to preach outside of the formula taught in class. Grasping for something to puff up my ego, I settle for not letting the Homiletics professor see me cry and promise myself that I will change things when I am serving in a parish. Although my classmates supported me after class, I wish someone had defended me while I was standing there knowing that I would cry if I tried to speak. I allowed myself to become trapped by an agreement that tears show weakness. There was no one, including myself willing to take the risk in front of the professor.

Entering the Truth Chamber: It is no one's job to defend me. I didn't even bother to stand up for myself. I was looking for outside affirmation from the professor and my classmates.

Intent: Faithfully preaching as inspired.

Re-entering the Truth Chamber: Preaching as inspired is not about outside affirmation. It is about faithfulness to the *in*spiration.

Re-entering the Story Chamber: I learned such a valuable lesson from this experience (even recapitulating it years later because of intervening experiences). My classmates cared for me as they were able, and I am grateful for their support. I've learned to share as inspired without seeking outside affirmation more and more often. Not seeking affirmation grows my active listening skills as people respond. I learn more and offer more this way.

Re-entering the Feeling Chamber: I feel strong and capable of growth.

For me, The Warrior Heart Practice feels like walking a labyrinth. I love labyrinths. We own a portable one that we share with the community. At times I dance through them feeling drawn to the center, which is akin to the Intent Chamber in Amara's paradigm. I always leave the center of a labyrinth with some form of enlightenment, which feels like focused Intent. The Truth of what I experienced unfolds in story as I remember it, or once again hear what I heard, as I make my way back to the beginning. As I turn to bow in reverence to the Mystery of it all, I always feel better and more whole. I turn again and walk away more capable of serving. I feel the same way running through The Warrior Heart Practice. It has become a valuable tool for me. I use it so often that when I start to feel triggered by anything, I automatically start walking through the chambers in my mind. Explore it and see what you think.[2]

THE GOSPEL OF MARY

The canon created at Emperor Constantine's request omitted Gnostic gospels based on inner knowing. Today we may describe this as intuitive knowing. Scholars believe that both women and men wrote, recorded, and copied these gospels. The canonized gospels objectify God as an entity outside of creation, which also leads to the objectification of women. Mary Magdalene is the quintessential example of this. Pope Gregory the Great's sermon portraying her as a prostitute set this in stone for over a thousand years. Search Mary Magdalene on TikTok and see what surfaces. Even after the catholic church apologized and declared a feast day for her, the damage continues.

The Gospel of Mary, an ancient Gnostic text attributed to Mary Magdalene, is the post canonical text we will consider with the Advent and Christmas canonical readings and throughout Year A of *The Revised Common Lectionary*. The gospel highlights the divine within all of creation while grounded in matter. Offsetting the spiritual energy losses suffered during the absence of both the Divine Feminine and consequently the compromised Sacred Masculine, it offers a highly significant vision for this time of transformation and transmutation.

POST-READING INTEGRATIONS

1. What disconnections do you experience in your life?

2. Recall an experience that continues to trigger you. Process it through The Warrior Heart Practice:

Entering the Feeling Chamber: How do you feel when you think about the situation?

walk within

Entering the Story Chamber: What happened in the situation?

Entering the Truth Chamber: What is true about the situation? (Simple words or phrases with no story attached).

Entering the Intent Chamber: What is your Intent? (Simple words or phrases).

Re-entering the Truth Chamber: Given your Intent, what is true about the situation?

Re-entering the Story Chamber: Given your Intent and Truth, what is your story about the situation?

Re-entering the Feeling Chamber: Given your Intent, Truth, and Story about the situation, how do you feel?

3. How does the idea of Mary Magdalene and Jesus being consorts impact your understanding of Divine Feminine and Sacred Masculine energies?

CHAPTER 3

Where do Bibles come from?

PRE-READING REFLECTIONS

1. Which, if any, bibles do you have access to in your home or online?

2. What is your current understanding of who wrote the bible?

3. Google the word "redaction" and describe it in your own words.

THE CHRISTIAN BIBLE

Composed of multiple books, the Christian bible comes in a variety of forms. Protestant bibles contain the First Testament Hebrew Bible and a Second Testament containing four gospels, Letters by Timothy and Paul, The Book of the Acts of the Apostles, and other books about the life and teachings of Jesus and his followers. The catholic bible contains these books and refers to them as the Vulgate. It also includes Apocrypha which are books and passages not included in protestant bibles.

Religious scholars greatly debate whether eyewitnesses of Jesus wrote the original gospel manuscripts since no historical evidence supports this. Questions surround what motivated the recording of the stories given the high cost of papyrus and historic oral tradition. Whatever our perspective on the stories of Jesus' crucifixion, death, and resurrection, it is important to understand that the church bases its perspective on a variety of hypotheses rather than facts. There are over 5,800 Greek Second Testament Manuscripts. These fragments are authenticated by copies found in Egypt. Only 11 of them are possibly considered first century texts. Fearing that carbon dating may damage the already fragile papyrus scrolls and booklets, researchers use paper type, ink, print, textual evidence, site of discovery, and other historical evidence to date manuscripts. At this point in time, we know of no original gospel texts, but only copies of copies of copies.

Church tradition states that the four canonical gospels are written by their namesakes. However, none of the gospels state the names of their authors, and there is no historical information identifying who wrote them. For the purpose of our Advent, Christmas, Solstice journeys, the information in the following chart helps guide us.

Where do Bibles come from?

Canonical Gospel	Hypothesized Origin Date and Earliest Hypothesized Manuscript	Hypothesized Reason for Recording	Curiosities
Mark: 1200 manuscripts. Mark's Jesus shows power over disease, evil nature, and death	70 CE Origin 138 CE Manuscript	Fall of the Jerusalem Temple	Begins with Jesus' baptism (no birth story), and the redacted ending involves the addition of Jesus appearing to the women at the tomb.
Matthew: 966 manuscripts. Matthew's Jesus is a King who comes to fulfill Messianic Law according to First Testament prophecies.	80-90 CE Origin 200 CE Manuscript	To encourage the Jewish Community to follow Jesus as the Messiah	Traditional birth story and resurrection. Dated later than Mark because similarities suggest author knew story of Mark, Luke, and what is hypothesized as a Q (unknown) source.
Luke: 182 manuscripts. Luke's Jesus is a perfect man who comes to save the world.	Later first century, approx. 85 CE Origin 175-225 CE Manuscript	For the Greek Gentiles concerned about how the government will view following Jesus	Scholars hypothesize that the author of Luke traveled with Paul and wrote the Book of Acts. Similarities suggest author of Luke knew story of Mark, Matthew, and what is hypothesized as a Q (unknown) source.

Canonical Gospel	Hypothesized Origin Date and Earliest Hypothesized Manuscript	Hypothesized Reason for Recording	Curiosities
John: 109 manuscripts. John's Jesus is the word of God incarnate living in the world	90-130 CE Origin 100-200 CE Manuscript	For the world when the Synagogue allegedly stated that the people had to choose between Jesus and the Synagogue and could no longer participate in both	Distinctly different from the other three gospels categorized as synoptic gospels. Hypothesized to be the last of the gospels recorded. Last in the canon, but archeological discoveries assure us that the gospel of John is NOT the last gospel recorded.

REDACTION AND INTERPRETATION OF MANUSCRIPTS

A review of biblical manuscripts reveals a variety of redactions. Redactions include edits and changes made from author to copier, author to translator, translator to copier, or copier to copier. It is easy to see how clerical changes occur when viewing original Greek texts on papyrus. Because papyrus was so valuable, there are no spaces between letters and no punctuation. Sometimes punctuation placement can change the meaning of a sentence. Differences between native languages can also impact redactions. While English defines words by context, biblical Greek uses different words to communicate connotations. There are 52 words for "love" in biblical Greek. This makes vocabulary study challenging.

Translation is more of an art than a science and is not as simple as a word-by-word, concrete, literal translation. Many variables impact it such as languages employing word order differently and changing values based on whether it is a time of abundance or famine. Translators' unique understanding of cultural norms will also impact their translations.

For instance, the oldest copies of Mark end with Jesus in the tomb. The resurrection story first appears in later gospels. This is a challenge for the church given the scholars' rule of thumb that the earliest versions are likely the most accurate. No resurrection in the earliest gospel undermines the church's story of Jesus. Scholars address the issue by suggesting that the gospel of Mark is a literary, rather than a historic, account of Jesus and eventually add a different ending. Most translations footnote this change.

Shifting pronoun references to the Holy Spirit also contribute to the role of the Divine Feminine. Original feminine references to the feminine Hebrew noun "Ruah" for Holy Spirit, were redacted to masculine pronoun references instead. Discovering this supports the re-emergence of the Divine Feminine as the references revert to the feminine again. While some scholars attempt to make a grammatical argument against this significance, stating that masculine, feminine, and neuter words do not necessarily follow human gender, they conclude that "god" has no gender.[3] This begs the question of whether to change the gender of pronoun references if this is the case. It also opens opportunities to reference "god" in the feminine—especially when earliest biblical references do so.

INCLUSIVE LANGUAGE

Inclusive language has become an ongoing consideration when translating. Research around a genderless "god" demonstrates patterns of harmony and wholeness within Divine Feminine and Sacred Masculine energies rather than simply integrated genders. As these realizations expand, translators redact gender pronoun references in favor of inclusive language.

CONTEMPORARY BIBLICAL LANGUAGE

Movements follow to contemporize biblical language. Eugene Peterson's biblical interpretation, *The Message,* is referenced as an "interpretation" because Peterson did not translate from biblical Hebrew and Greek texts to create the contemporary language employed in his work. It is important to consider options, so I encourage you to explore this interpretation with a translation from the biblical languages as it yields another perspective. To this end, I include both a biblical language translation and Peterson's contemporary interpretation for each gospel reading that we consider. I frequently used *The Message* while preaching and found it to be a valuable resource. Readers new to the bible may find it especially helpful.

ARCHEOLOGICAL RESEARCH

While consulting at The Art Institute of Chicago, I learned a great deal about the finances, discovery, and curation of art. In 2000, the Pharaohs of the Sun (Akhenaten, Nefertiti, Tutankhamen) exhibit from the Museum of Fine Arts, Boston arrived in Chicago. Akhenaten allowed Egyptian artists to portray things as they appeared in nature rather than according to a strict formula for the first time in Egyptian history. The exhibit contained hundreds of sculpted busts to show the variety that emerged. The display included a controversial bust of Nefertiti.

Most archeologists need patrons. Countries invest based on the anticipated importance of discoveries. The investors split the finds according to investment. In this manner, Germany acquired a bust of Nefertiti requiring restoration. The controversy surrounds how the restoration took place. Critics claim a highly westernized version of Nefertiti emerged rather than an Egyptian one. Stories of Nefertiti's beauty spanned thousands of years. In a western colonized world, it appears the restorers believed that beauty needed to mirror itself.

Similar issues arise with ancient manuscripts. Archeologists did not initially make the two most recent discoveries of Nag Hammadi texts (1945) and the Dead Sea Scrolls (1947). The young people shepherding nearby and playing in the caves brought them home or to the market. Once authenticated, archeologists arrived financed by interested groups. The Dead Sea Scrolls first came into public view in 1990. All kinds of theories developed around what took so long. Great public interest greeted their release. The scrolls contain First Testament texts, and the church announced, with relief, no major biblical differences.

However, as Dead Sea Scrolls scholar, Lawrence Schiffman observes, "Perhaps the most important of all, we come to understand the plurality and variety of interpretations of the Bible and the manner in which they would shape that later development of religious traditions."[4] He further explains," . . . one can trace so many details of agreement and disagreement between groups, clear examples of Judaism and inter-group tension, that there is simply no comparison between what we know now and what was known before the scrolls were made available to us."[5] Considering a variety of perspectives stands at the heart of Judaism. As a result of discovering the scrolls between April 29 and May 3, 2018, the Jewish Learning Institute began offering a course in 400 locations titled "Great Debates in Jewish History."

The Nag Hammadi Gnostic texts entered the public view gradually as codices were initially sold to the highest bidders. The most famous of these was the codex gifted to Carl Jung for his birthday. "Jung's death in 1961 resulted in a quarrel over the ownership of the Jung Codex; the pages were not given to the Coptic Museum in Cairo until 1975, after a first edition of the text had been published."[6] By 2001, all of the Nag Hammadi texts were rejoined and translated for public consumption. Intervening conferences convened to determine a scholarly definition of "Gnostic." The agreed upon definition is "finding god through inner wisdom."

Unlike the Dead Sea Scrolls, the Nag Hammadi texts were previously identified as heretical and marginalized when Emperor Constantine sought a canon. When rediscovered and translated, they were once again marginalized by the church and remain labeled unorthodox today. Contemporary Christianity does not host "Great Debates in Christian History" like the Jewish Learning Institute held in response to the discovery of the Dead Sea Scrolls. Contemporary Christianity seeks to identify the correct idea of God rather than seeking meaning in discovered texts. It views meaning as static and set in stone. If discovered texts do not fit this truth, they are discarded rather than considered for what meaning they might add to the story of Jesus. Readers must consciously choose to integrate these texts into their perspectives.

PERSPECTIVE, AGENDA, AND DOGMA

Everyone has a perspective. Our perspectives are based on agreements that we make with ourselves and the world. We must ask ourselves if we take responsibility for our lives or if we expect others or institutions to be responsible for them. Religious dogma teaches that, unless participants believe what the church denomination teaches, they are not members. Becoming a member typically involves giving away one's own perspective and vowing to take on the church denomination's perspective. A denomination's perspective is set by its agenda.

ORDAINING GAY CLERGY ILLUSTRATION

The issue of ordaining gay clergy illustrates the relationship between perspective, agenda, and dogma. When I attended seminary, I facilitated the Shower of Stoles exhibit on campus. It contains over 1,000 stoles and other items from LGBTQ people active in their faith communities from 32 denominations in six countries. The most moving items are the letters written by clergy members who were defrocked because of their sexual orientation or committed suicide because they could not answer their calls to ministry. This exhibit traveled the nation as church bodies wrestled with the question of ordaining gay clergy.

Many church denominations teach that homosexuality is a sin according to concrete, literal interpretations of the bible. Historical information about Jesus, as well as material world context, began to challenge this dogma and allowed for shifts in perspective to occur. This brought the question before church denominations at their national gatherings.

When the largest and most progressive Lutheran denomination voted to ordain gay pastors, it lost many members. This resulted, in part at least, from neglecting to address the conditions of a previous merger. That merger allowed congregations that entered the merger with property to leave with that property. When some decided to continue believing what the church previously taught them, their congregations took their buildings with them and departed. This led to a crisis within the body and the denomination attempted to realign itself by allowing individual congregations to determine if they would call gay pastors.

Observing what happened in the ELCA, the Episcopal church set an agenda to avoid fracturing. This involved an archdiocese-by-archdiocese decision to call and ordain gay clergy members. When the first gay bishop was elected to lead the divided archdioceses, the conflict expanded internationally. "For the first time, the global organizing body of Anglicans punished the Episcopal Church, following years of heated debate with the American church over homosexuality, same-sex marriage and the role of women."[7]

Most recently, the Methodist church postponed a quadrennial General Conference discussion about a planned division of the United Methodist Church until 2024 due to the pandemic. Frustrated by the delay, those opposed to ordaining gay clergy and same-sex marriage left the body and created the Global Methodist Church in June 2022. This leaves the remaining United Methodist church members to find a path forward. That path will most likely be formalized in 2024.

STRUGGLING WITH CHANGE

Ironically the Christian Church has no means to address shifts in perspective, despite the biblical Jesus being an inspiring changemaker. Majority votes in congregations do not change hearts any more than governmental legislation does. I recall sitting in a bible study with church leaders regarding the ordination of women. Such studies are often filled with information explaining that bible passages do not mean what they literally say. One leader asked, "How do I address the way I treated my wife and daughter all these years according to what the church previously taught?"

I finally understood why change in the church is so difficult. If people give away their decision-making authority to the church and live their relationships according to church teachings, how do they get "do overs" when the church changes its teachings? Unconditional love and remembering that we do not know what we do not know can help heal wounds. They highlight how retaining responsibility for our lives, acquiring skills to entertain a variety of perspectives, and unlearning dogma that separates rather than connects are important parts of a walk within.

NEUROSCIENCE

Neuroscience teaches us more and more each day about how our brains function. How our brains work also impacts redaction, translation, and interpretation. All of these inform the bibles we hold in our hands and our understanding of them. Historically, people have been identified as either right- or left-brained. In his work, *The Master and His Emissary*, Iain McGilchrist describes a more fluid human brain at work. He suggests that information and experiences enter our brains through our right hemispheres, move to our left hemispheres for consideration and organization, and return to the right hemisphere for disbursement through action. I imagine it as something like a waltz. 1-2-3, 1-2-3, right-left-right, right-left-right.

When information, experiences, and feelings remain in the left hemisphere and do not return to the right hemisphere, we become static, judgmental, and unable to grow. This is why the work of ongoing embodiment and contemplation of agreements is essential. It helps draw the information back to the right hemisphere for empathetic application by context rather than judgmental self-righteousness. This process engages us in an ongoing co-creative process of meaning making.

STATIC OR DYNAMIC PERSPECTIVES?

Essentially, we find ourselves at points of choice when we read bibles. Do we read them to affirm what we have previously heard or learned? If they do not fit prescribed dogma, do we dismiss them as heretical? Do we read them engaging our growing experience in the world? Do we understand Jesus as static or dynamic? Does our understanding of Jesus evolve as we access new information about him and the world in which he lived? As we access new information about the world in which we live?

Neuroscience and Quantum Physics suggest that dynamic, rather than static, perspectives promote mindfulness, wellness, and healing. Acknowledging our co-creative roles in the meaning of our lives allows us to learn from mistakes. Rather than being stuck in guilt and shame that inhibits self-esteem, we freely show up to serve.

POST-READING INTEGRATIONS

1. Describe something that you have unlearned.

2. Of the variables explored, which are the most significant to your understanding of where bibles come from?

3. What static and dynamic perspectives do you hold?

CHAPTER 4

The Revised Common Lectionary–Passages for the Journey

PRE-READING REFLECTIONS

1. What are your thoughts, feelings, and beliefs about God/Creator/Beloved/Source/Spirit/Wholeness/Mystery/Energy/(Other) _____?

2. If you experience God/Creator/Beloved/Source/Spirit/Wholeness/Mystery/Energy/(Other)_____, what does the experience look and feel like for you?

3. Do you find any biblical passages meaningful? If so, which ones? How have you applied them in your life?

THE REVISED COMMON LECTIONARY

There are many ways to coordinate passages from the canonized gospels and rediscovered post canonical gospels. Christianity historically influenced America through its inception and institutions and influenced the western world through colonization. In this manner, even non-Christians are impacted by its teachings. Rather than a random correlation, or one that may serve the post canonical gospels' agendas, this series employs the passages shared in Christian churches on Sundays called the Revised Common Lectionary (RCL).

The RCL is a three-year cycle of weekly readings used by the vast majority of mainline Protestant churches in Canada and the United States. During most of the year, the readings include: a passage from the Hebrew Bible, a Psalm, a passage from Letters attributed to Paul, and a Gospel reading.

The seasons of the Church Year are said to reflect the life of Christ: Advent, Christmas, Epiphany, Lent, Easter, and Ordinary Time. Consequently, the Sunday gospel readings provide weekly focus. The gospel readings for each year come from one of the synoptic gospels according to the following pattern: Year A: Matthew, Year B: Mark, and Year C: Luke. Readings from the Gospel of John can be found throughout the RCL with a conscious attempt to include a reading from John each month.

The Revised Common Lectionary, first published in 1992, derives from The Common Lectionary of 1983. Both were based on a post-Vatican II revision of the Roman Lectionary. "The post-Vatican II Roman Lectionary represented a profound break with the past. Not only were the readings organized according to a plan whereby a richer fare of scripture was read in liturgical celebrations, in contrast to the medieval lectionary where the choice of readings was simply helter-skelter, but for the first time in history the Sunday lectionary covered a period of three years, each year being dedicated to a particular synoptic author--Matthew, Mark, or Luke."[8]

Historically, the RCL integrates both protestant and catholic Sunday church readings. This enables an ecumenical discussion of the texts by those who hear them in church on Sundays. Sharing them in this series hopefully expands an opportunity for contemplation and discussion with those of us not attending Sunday services. Learn more about the RCL at **lectionary.library.vanderbilt.edu/faq2.php.** This library monitors the RCL and will respond to specific questions and inquiries.

Readings for any given Sunday generally have a thematic relationship to the gospel reading for that day, although this is not always the case. They are noted in this series each week for readers to explore as desired. All the readings shared come from the New International Version translation of the Bible. It is arguably the most gender inclusive translation thus far. This inclusivity involves references to people more than references to God.

HOW DO WE UNDERSTAND THE WORD "GOD"?

It is up to us, as humans, to determine how we understand God. Since Christianity hinges its story on the Hebrew Torah and the rest of the First Testament by claiming Jesus as the fulfillment of another faith group's story, it is significant to understand how that group understood God. A scholar of Christian origins and gender theory reports, "The personal name of God, 'Yahweh,' which is revealed to Moses in Exodus 3, is a remarkable combination of both female and male grammatical endings. The first part of God's name in Hebrew, 'Yah,' is feminine and the last part, 'weh,' is masculine. Considering this, feminist theologian, Mary Daly asks, 'Why must 'God' be a noun? Why not a verb—the most active and dynamic of all?'"[9] The Hebrew bible does not assign God a gender but integrates masculine and feminine energies within God. Since energy is dynamic rather than static, both Daly's question and assertion deserve serious consideration as we examine our own understandings of God.

The series also includes each week's gospel text from *The Message* as well. This is an interpretation of the bible that uses the most contemporary language. While I cannot include all of the possible translations, please consider this link for additional translations in 74 languages **biblegateway.com**. Use these passages or any translation—whichever works best for you.

THE GOSPEL OF MARY

Given the marginalization of the Divine Feminine for thousands of years, *The Gospel of Mary* appropriately stands as the first re-discovered, post canonical text for consideration with the canonical gospels. A variety of translations with historical research exist. Given the brief length of the gospel, it is possible to review several translations and witness the variety within them. This gospel serves as a wonderful snapshot of the variables informing translation. I offer classes exploring this further.

For the purposes of this walk, I selected Mark M. Mattison's free online translation at **gospels.net/mary**. Please start with a translation that suits your journey. This fascinating gnostic text is only 18 pages long, with the most complete copy missing pages at the beginning as well as another four pages missing later in the text. The remaining pages give us insights regarding a visionary walk within as well as the patriarchy's response to that journey.

EARTH BASED PERSPECTIVE

It is important to note that, while the church calendar claims to base itself on the life of Christ, it also mirrors the seasons of the year. Throughout time, Indigenous peoples based their practices on the seasons as well. Rejected as polytheists, we learn more and more each day about the spirit within all of creation honored by these peoples. There is no birth date recorded for Jesus, but the church places it near the Winter solstice. The Solstice celebrates the transition from the shortest day/longest night to the return of more light.

Jesus' Easter resurrection follows the pattern of new life documented by spring. In the battle of religions, conquerors often usurped the practices of the conquered to show supremacy and dominance.

Given the code red climate change and world pandemics that we face today, our journey will stop to contemplate the Earth's perspective regarding the passages that we consider. How might we give up the pursuit of dominion over the earth? The original Hebrew in the book of Genesis directs humans to live co-creatively with all sentient beings on earth and not with any sense of superiority. However, English translations report "man having dominion over the beasts of the field, the birds of the air, and the fish of the sea" following the story of Noah and the flood in Genesis 9.

A need for superiority led to disrupting, disconnecting, and discarding relationships with other species and their energies that can help us manage balance. To regain balance and harmony we must develop *the ears to hear and eyes to see* that Jesus describes. Unfortunately, we have previously understood this wisdom in a limited human context. A walk within requires time to grow and to understand it in the context of all sentient beings including Mother Earth's perspective.

TRANSPARENCY

The variables identified in the previous four chapters are ones that I consciously acknowledge as impacting my agreements. They do not represent an exhaustive list but offer a place to start. The variables that impact my agreements, may not be the same ones that impact yours. My hope is that considering them may help bring variables that do impact your agreements to the surface for your consideration.

Enjoy hospitality and community along the journey through weekly zoom gatherings. Visit **crystalsteinbergcocreating.com** *for more information.*

POST-READING INTEGRATIONS

1. Have you ever discussed a bible passage or a bible story with anyone outside of a church setting? If so, which one? What did the discussion involve? If you had multiple conversations, which one was the most meaningful?

2. Note what you know and how you know (intuitively, through dreams, feelings, and readings outside of the bible, etc.) about God at this point in the journey?

3. Describe your relationship with the earth and all that is in it.

4. List any variables already coming to mind that impact your agreements about God and religion.

CHAPTER 5

What is Coming?
Year A: Advent I

PRE-READING REFLECTIONS

1. Today's gospel reading describes keeping watch. Under what circumstances do you feel a need to keep watch?

2. List what you know about the story of Noah's ark and how you learned what you know.

What I know about Noah's Ark...	How I learned this...

3. What does the phrase "the Son of Man" imply to you?

FIRST TESTAMENT READING FROM ISAIAH 2: 1-5

This is what Isaiah, son of Amos saw concerning Judah and Jerusalem:

² In the last days
the mountain of the Lord's temple will be established
   as the highest of the mountains;
it will be exalted above the hills,
   and all nations will stream to it.
³ Many peoples will come and say,
"Come, let us go up to the mountain of the Lord,
   to the temple of the God of Jacob.
He will teach us his ways,
   so that we may walk in his paths."
The law will go out from Zion,
   the word of the Lord from Jerusalem.
⁴ He will judge between the nations
   and will settle disputes for many peoples.
They will beat their swords into plowshares
   and their spears into pruning hooks.
Nation will not take up sword against nation,
   nor will they train for war anymore.
⁵ Come, descendants of Jacob,
   let us walk in the light of the Lord.

NOTES

A READING FROM PSALM 122

¹ I rejoiced with those who said to me,
   "Let us go to the house of the Lord."
² Our feet are standing
   in your gates, Jerusalem.
³ Jerusalem is built like a city
   that is closely compacted together.
⁴ That is where the tribes go up—
   the tribes of the Lord—
to praise the name of the Lord
   according to the statute given to Israel.
⁵ There stand the thrones for judgment,
   the thrones of the house of David.
⁶ Pray for the peace of Jerusalem:
   "May those who love you be secure.
⁷ May there be peace within your walls
   and security within your citadels."
⁸ For the sake of my family and friends,
   I will say, "Peace be within you."
⁹ For the sake of the house of the Lord our God,
   I will seek your prosperity.

NOTES

A READING FROM PAUL'S LETTER TO THE ROMANS 13: 11-14

¹¹And do this, understanding the present time: The hour has already come for you to wake up from your slumber, because our salvation is nearer now than when we first believed. ¹² The night is nearly over; the day is almost here. So let us put aside the deeds of darkness and put on the armor of light. ¹³ Let us behave decently, as in the daytime, not in carousing and drunkenness, not in sexual immorality and debauchery, not in dissension and jealousy. ¹⁴ Rather, clothe yourselves with the Lord Jesus Christ, and do not think about how to gratify the desires of the flesh.

NOTES

A READING FROM MATTHEW 24: 36-44
(NIV INCLUSIVE LANGUAGE TRANSLATION)

[36] "But about that day or hour no one knows, not even the angels in heaven, nor the Son,[a] but only the Father. [37] As it was in the days of Noah, so it will be at the coming of the Son of Man. [38] For in the days before the flood, people were eating and drinking, marrying and giving in marriage, up to the day Noah entered the ark; [39] and they knew nothing about what would happen until the flood came and took them all away. That is how it will be at the coming of the Son of Man. [40] Two men will be in the field; one will be taken and the other left. [41] Two women will be grinding with a hand mill; one will be taken and the other left.

[42] "Therefore keep watch, because you do not know on what day your Lord will come. [43] But understand this: If the owner of the house had known at what time of night the thief was coming, he would have kept watch and would not have let his house be broken into. [44] So you also must be ready, because the Son of Man will come at an hour when you do not expect him.

NOTES

A READING FROM MATTHEW 24: 36-44
(MSG CONTEMPORARY LANGUAGE INTERPRETATION)

[36] "But the exact day and hour? No one knows that, not even heaven's angels, not even the Son. Only the Father knows.

[37-39] "The Arrival of the Son of Man will take place in times like Noah's. Before the great flood everyone was carrying on as usual, having a good time right up to the day Noah boarded the ark. They knew nothing—until the flood hit and swept everything away.

[39-44] "The Son of Man's Arrival will be like that: Two men will be working in the field—one will be taken, one left behind; two women will be grinding at the mill—one will be taken, one left behind. So stay awake, alert. You have no idea what day your Master will show up. But you do know this: You know that if the homeowner had known what time of night the burglar would arrive, he would have been there with his dogs to prevent the break-in. Be vigilant just like that. You have no idea when the Son of Man is going to show up.

NOTES

CONTEMPLATING THE GOSPEL OF MATTHEW

The word "advent" comes from the Latin word for coming: "adventus." Immediately, we may wonder what is coming. The church directs us to ask *who* is coming. The answer in the canonical gospels is Jesus, in terms of either birth or second coming. Matthew clearly communicates this. The analogy to Noah's ark, the flood, and the unprepared people suggest some type of danger associated with the coming of the Son of Man. The disappearance of one of the men working in the field and one of the women grinding at the mill is reminiscent of *The Left Behind* series by Tim LaHaye and Jerry Jenkins (1995-2007). Be vigilant and act properly or be left behind is the message often taught and preached from Matthew's gospel.

In fairness to the author(s) of Matthew, the hypothesized time of writing follows the second destruction of the Jerusalem temple and questions that consequently emerged. Sacred ancient texts were no more written in a vacuum than anything is today. They had a context. With the fall of the temple came questions about what it meant to be Jewish, whether non-Jews could be Christians, and how Jews and Christians might interrelate.

Paul's letters, dated by scholars as the earliest Christian writings, included Jews and non-Jews alike. It was important to Paul that followers of Jesus be able to attend synagogue, maintain Jewish traditions, and follow Jesus while also welcoming non-Jews as followers of Jesus. The second fall of the Jerusalem temple in 70 CE challenged this perspective. The community, led by the author(s) of Matthew, maintained hospitality for Jews and non-Jews alike. However, becoming a Christian meant no longer following Jewish traditions. The return of Jesus that was considered imminent required full faithfulness to Jesus, alone, to demonstrate one's role within the elect.

MY PERSONAL EXPERIENCES

In Matthew, readers see fear of being left behind or left out. Isn't that a fear within all of us? The reason so many of us remain in unhealthy situations? Out of fear of what is coming if we don't abide by cultural norms and societal rules? For me, this involved the vow I made to God, the church, and God's people to serve them.

I went on leave from call to be my mother's primary caregiver when she received a terminal diagnosis. During this time, I facilitated my mom living while actively dying as much as possible. At the same time, I started taking care of myself by swimming, attending yoga classes, and finding a nutritional program that worked for me. I didn't want her to worry about me after she was gone. I wanted her to know that I would be okay. My mom was able to cheer me on as she watched me participate in a triathlon for the first time.

Her death opened a portal to many mystical experiences. She died at 2:30 am. When I called my partner to tell him, he was at the front door with electricians. The fuse box on the corner of our lot had exploded at the same time she died. The electricians arrived to say that they would return the next day to trim trees that presented a fire hazard given these events. None of us would have noticed the hazard without the explosion in the fuse box.

After my mom died, I continued training. I felt the best that I had felt in my entire life and found myself arranging healing programs for my husband's clients. I was strong and healthy. When the deadline drew near for determining if I would return to church service, I went on a month-long retreat to listen. I had faced my terrible self-care habits. For the most part, the church pays lip service to self-care and provides little support for it.

Typically, women are placed in small, dying congregations that struggle to survive, require hospice chaplains as they die, and can't afford to pay their pastors due to low offerings despite their best intentions. Women serving the church are 47% more likely to require mental health care.[10] I watched sisters resign from the pulpit during worship service, succumb to mental illness, and die from health ailments while serving.

Unwilling to make such a sacrifice for the church and not believing that Jesus desired such sacrifices, I reviewed the church's foundational documents. I could not find the word "healing" anywhere. The absence of the word amazed me. I shared this with church leaders when we met to discuss my potential return. They suggested that I chair a Healing Round Table. My duties would include driving between two states to be sure congregational leaders completed their annual Mayo clinic surveys. This would ensure that the church received a discount on its health insurance premiums.

Returning to my personal retreat and considering the church's offer, I realized that ensuring discounts on health insurance premiums was not my calling. I started rewriting the foundational documents of the church to include healing when a voice in my head said, "This is not going to change them."

"Maybe not right away, but if I chair the round table, perhaps eventually," my heart replied.

"And how has that worked out for you in the past?" my integrated HeartMind inquired.

"Not that well," I had to admit. I called it the nodding of the head syndrome—agreement when hearing new ideas followed by heads shaking 'no' if the new ideas required changing anything. I decided to take a break.

A MYSTICAL EXPERIENCE

I walked out of my place and drove to a neighborhood rummage in a subdivision that I had never entered before. At the first stop, I saw four placemats with gallery art on them: Vincent Van Gogh's *Sunflowers*, Paul Gauguin's *Vision After the Sermon*, Claude Monet's *Waterlilies*, and Mary Cassatt's *The Child's Bath*.

"What a coincidence, I saw all four of these pieces uncrated for exhibits at The Art Institute of Chicago when I consulted there," I said to the woman behind the table.

"Do you like art?" the homeowner asked. "Come inside and see what I did to the walls."

Following her into the house, I saw the Arizona mountain scape on the living room walls. "Beautiful," I started saying, but then, suddenly, I felt as if an arm was around my waist and another was slung over my shoulder by my neck. Tears flowed as I apologized to my host. "I am so sorry, but I feel like someone is hugging me around my waist and shoulders."

"Oh, that's Raphael. He came to bring your mother for a visit today," she replied without any hesitation. I had never met this woman, had not told her about my mother's death, and had to ask how she knew this.

"I am told," she said. "That's why I painted the mountains on my walls. All souls meet here. Now take a minute to enjoy your visit."

I closed my eyes and stood there smiling for I do not know how long. I could not help crying, but I felt so happy at the same time. When the hugging feeling stopped, I opened my eyes to find myself standing alone in the room. "Thank you," I called into the house.

"Love you," came the response that sounded like my mother as I opened the door to exit. What does one do when, instead of feeling excluded, as anticipated, one is included? Included in the awareness of the universe? It is life changing. I had left my house frustrated in my attempt to change others. Now I felt energized and inspired to follow my calling wherever it led simply because it is my calling. I no longer needed the church to change in order to answer it.

When I returned to my desk, I reviewed the draft of the church's foundational documents that I began re-writing prior to the mystical experience at the rummage sale. It no longer applied. I had to leave the roster and follow this new awareness. I began my resignation letter. Tears flowed from my eyes as I wondered if I was doing the right thing, what people would think of me, and what lay ahead.

In one way or another, I had been serving the church my entire life. For me, leaving the roster also meant leaving the church. While some place deep inside of me knew I would not spontaneously combust and go to hell, it was sad and scary, but also enlivening. That mystical experience changed everything in a moment and gave me the courage to stand in the Mystery despite my fears.

THE GOSPEL OF MARY: PAGE 7

"Then will matter be destroyed or not?"

The Savior said, "Every nature, every form, every creature exists in and with each other, but they'll dissolve again into their own roots, because the nature of matter dissolves into its nature alone. Anyone who has ears to hear should hear."

NOTES

CONTEMPLATING *THE GOSPEL OF MARY*

When I left the roster, everything was up for review—to be recapitulated in the Toltec sense of reviewing what I knew and how I knew it. What do I know rather than believe? How do I know it? How does each experience impact my knowing? How am I in relationship with others and their knowings? Things previously shunned by church dogma became open to investigation. *The Gospel of Mary* is one of these things.

Church History class in seminary assessed our abilities to list heresies challenging the Christian faith. Knowing the divine through inner wisdom such as the Gnostic gospels was one of the heresies listed. The connectedness that *The Gospel of Mary* describes frees me to explore these heresies. I find a different Jesus in these texts. Not a Jesus who I must fear discovering my imperfections and who will consequently leave me behind, but one who shares the connection to "Every nature, every form, every creature existing with each other." If everything is connected, I cannot be left out. Nothing is left out. If "Everything dissolves again into their roots," that includes me and all that exists. All connects to the origins of matter. This underscores walks within to identify the Wisdom that we each carry.

WHAT IF?

Leaving the church roster found me exploring who Jesus is without the dogma. I have this knowing that the essence of Jesus stands accessible no matter what dogma has been created through interpretation, preaching, and councils. Reconsidering canonical texts alongside non-canonical texts expands our awareness through synthesis. For instance, in the gospel of Matthew passage considered this week, what if the two men in the field and the two women at the mill are different aspects of one man and one woman? What if no longer living in a dualistic paradigm of good and bad frees us to become whole? What if, in that wholeness, we greet and co-create with the Son of Man and Mary Magdalene who are also connected? What kind of world will this become if it is such Wholeness that Advent brings?

POST-READING INTEGRATIONS

1. Describe any coincidental, synchronistic, and/or mystical experience of significance in your life.

2. What is coming up in you this advent season?

3. List any knowings that you are reconsidering and/or discovering given what is coming up inside of you.

CHAPTER 6

What if there is no sin?
Year A: Advent Week II

PRE-READING REFLECTIONS

1. Have you been baptized or experienced/witnessed any purification rituals? Describe your experience(s).

2. What have you previously learned about John the Baptist? How did you learn these things?

Things I learned about John the Baptist...	How I came to understand this...

3. Describe your understanding of the word "sin." How did you arrive at this understanding?

FIRST TESTAMENT READING FROM ISAIAH 11: 1-10

¹ A shoot will come up from the stump of Jesse;
  from his roots a Branch will bear fruit.
² The Spirit of the Lord will rest on him—
  the Spirit of wisdom and of understanding,
  the Spirit of counsel and of might,
  the Spirit of the knowledge and fear of the Lord—
³ and he will delight in the fear of the Lord.
He will not judge by what he sees with his eyes,
  or decide by what he hears with his ears;
⁴ but with righteousness he will judge the needy,
  with justice he will give decisions for the poor of the earth.
He will strike the earth with the rod of his mouth;
  with the breath of his lips he will slay the wicked.
⁵ Righteousness will be his belt
  and faithfulness the sash around his waist.
⁶ The wolf will live with the lamb,
  the leopard will lie down with the goat,
the calf and the lion and the yearling[a] together;
  and a little child will lead them.
⁷ The cow will feed with the bear,
  their young will lie down together,
  and the lion will eat straw like the ox.
⁸ The infant will play near the cobra's den,
  and the young child will put its hand into the viper's nest.
⁹ They will neither harm nor destroy
  on all my holy mountain,
for the earth will be filled with the knowledge of the Lord
  as the waters cover the sea.
¹⁰ In that day the Root of Jesse will stand as a banner for the peoples; the nations will rally to him, and his resting place will be glorious.

What if there is no sin? Year A: Advent Week II

NOTES

READING FROM PSALM 72: 1-7

¹ Endow the king with your justice, O God,
  the royal son with your righteousness.
² May he judge your people in righteousness,
  your afflicted ones with justice.
³ May the mountains bring prosperity to the people,
  the hills the fruit of righteousness.
⁴ May he defend the afflicted among the people
  and save the children of the needy;
  may he crush the oppressor.
⁵ May he endure[a] as long as the sun,
  as long as the moon, through all generations.
⁶ May he be like rain falling on a mown field,
  like showers watering the earth.
⁷ In his days may the righteous flourish
  and prosperity abound till the moon is no more.

NOTES

A SECOND TESTAMENT READING FROM PAUL'S LETTER TO THE ROMANS 15: 4-13

For everything that was written in the past was written to teach us, so that through the endurance taught in the Scriptures and the encouragement they provide we might have hope. ⁵ May the God who gives endurance and encouragement give you the same attitude of mind toward each other that Christ Jesus had, ⁶ so that with one mind and one voice you may glorify the God and Father of our Lord Jesus Christ.
⁷ Accept one another, then, just as Christ accepted you, in order to bring praise to God. ⁸ For I tell you that Christ has become a servant of the Jews[a] on behalf of God's truth, so that the promises made to the patriarchs might be confirmed ⁹ and, moreover, that the Gentiles might glorify God for his mercy. As it is written:
"Therefore I will praise you among the Gentiles;
   I will sing the praises of your name."[b]
¹⁰ Again, it says,
"Rejoice, you Gentiles, with his people."[c]
¹¹ And again,
"Praise the Lord, all you Gentiles;
   let all the peoples extol him."[d]
¹² And again, Isaiah says,
"The Root of Jesse will spring up,
   one who will arise to rule over the nations;
   in him the Gentiles will hope."[e]
¹³ May the God of hope fill you with all joy and peace as you trust in him, so that you may overflow with hope by the power of the Holy Spirit.

NOTES

READING FROM MATTHEW 3: 1-12 (NIV)

3 In those days John the Baptist came, preaching in the wilderness of Judea ² and saying, "Repent, for the kingdom of heaven has come near." ³ This is he who was spoken of through the prophet Isaiah:
"A voice of one calling in the wilderness,
'Prepare the way for the Lord,
   make straight paths for him.'"[a]
⁴ John's clothes were made of camel's hair, and he had a leather belt around his waist. His food was locusts and wild honey. ⁵ People went out to him from Jerusalem and all Judea and the whole region of the Jordan. ⁶ Confessing their sins, they were baptized by him in the Jordan River.

⁷ But when he saw many of the Pharisees and Sadducees coming to where he was baptizing, he said to them: "You brood of vipers! Who warned you to flee from the coming wrath? ⁸ Produce fruit in keeping with repentance. ⁹ And do not think you can say to yourselves, 'We have Abraham as our father.' I tell you that out of these stones God can raise up children for Abraham. ¹⁰ The ax is already at the root of the trees, and every tree that does not produce good fruit will be cut down and thrown into the fire.

¹¹ "I baptize you with[b] water for repentance. But after me comes one who is more powerful than I, whose sandals I am not worthy to carry. He will baptize you with[c] the Holy Spirit and fire. ¹² His winnowing fork is in his hand, and he will clear his threshing floor, gathering his wheat into the barn and burning up the chaff with unquenchable fire."

What if there is no sin? Year A: Advent Week II

NOTES

READING FROM MATTHEW 3: 1-12 (MSG)

3 ¹⁻² While Jesus was living in the Galilean hills, John, called "the Baptizer," was preaching in the desert country of Judea. His message was simple and austere, like his desert surroundings: "Change your life. God's kingdom is here."

³ John and his message were authorized by Isaiah's prophecy:
Thunder in the desert!
Prepare for God's arrival!
Make the road smooth and straight!

⁴⁻⁶ John dressed in a camel-hair habit tied at the waist by a leather strap. He lived on a diet of locusts and wild field honey. People poured out of Jerusalem, Judea, and the Jordanian countryside to hear and see him in action. There at the Jordan River those who came to confess their sins were baptized into a changed life.

⁷⁻¹⁰ When John realized that a lot of Pharisees and Sadducees were showing up for a baptismal experience because it was becoming the popular thing to do, he exploded: "Brood of snakes! What do you think you're doing slithering down here to the river? Do you think a little water on your snakeskins is going to make any difference? It's your life that must change, not your skin! And don't think you can pull rank by claiming Abraham as father. Being a descendant of Abraham is neither here nor there. Descendants of Abraham are a dime a dozen. What counts is your life. Is it green and flourishing? Because if it's deadwood, it goes on the fire.

¹¹⁻¹² "I'm baptizing you here in the river, turning your old life in for a kingdom life. The real action comes next: The main character in this drama—compared to him I'm a mere stagehand—will ignite the kingdom life within you, a fire within you, the Holy Spirit within you, changing you from the inside out. He's going to clean house—make a clean sweep of your lives. He'll place everything true in its proper place before God; everything false he'll put out with the trash to be burned."

NOTES

CONTEMPLATING THE GOSPEL OF MATTHEW

This gospel highlights baptism again, while the first gospel lesson of Advent engages fear, the second Advent reading involves guilt and shame. There was plenty of guilt and shame to go around long before the story of John the Baptist preparing the way for Jesus. Throughout time, humans sought to purify themselves through human sacrifices, animal sacrifices, shamanic ceremonies, ritual baths, and baptism. Baptism, which means immersion, is not a Christian invention. The baptism that John performs in the desert grows out of a Jewish tradition of purification. "By the time of Christ, ceremonial cleanliness by water had become institutionalized into a purity ritual involving full immersion in a mikveh (or miqveh), a "collection of water." Mikveh purification was required of all Jews before they could enter the Temple or participate in major festivals."[11] The unknown author(s) of the gospel of Matthew adopts baptism as a central theme for preparing the people to receive Jesus. This involves repentance from sins.

Baptism is highlighted again in this gospel when Jesus comes to be baptized by John, but John does not feel worthy to baptize Jesus. Jesus' baptism can be a quandary for religious scholars because, if baptism involves repentance of sins and Jesus has no sin, why does John baptize him? The author(s) of Matthew answers this question with the last words of the gospel that have come to be known as "The Great Commission." "Therefore, go and make disciples of all nations, baptizing them in the name of the Father and of the Son and of the Holy Spirit, and teaching them to obey everything I have commanded you. And surely, I am with you always, to the very end of the age" (28: 19-20). Jesus' baptism signals an anointing of Jesus as Messiah and, eventually, a Christian savior.

Navigating these two worlds challenges the early church. As a Lutheran, we were trained to confirm Second Testament teachings with First Testament texts. I was in seminary before it dawned on me that the Second Testament authors knew and used copies of First Testament texts while authoring the Second Testament. This allowed the identification of Jesus as the fulfillment of the First Testament Hebrew scriptures to encourage Jews as well as gentiles to follow Jesus. In large ways, this is a quintessential example of cultural appropriation. How do Jews believe that Jesus is the Messiah whose tasks include freeing the Israelites from gentiles but also welcome gentiles to follow Jesus? The need for freedom from sin and shame through a baptism pointing to the Messianic Savior known as Jesus integrated the two paths.

This combination is part of what leads to Constantine demanding a canon. Just who is this Jesus? How can the gentile savior be the Jewish Messiah? But the result of this canonization generates a static, rather than a dynamic, Jesus and limits humanity to contexts thousands of years old. Limitation lowers vibration. Being tied to the past rather than open to discoveries minimizes our ability to be present in the moment. This leads to inflexibility and horrors such as the destruction of the Alexandrian library, the destruction of anything other than canonical gospels, crusades, inquisitions, dictatorships, and insurrections. Our DNA carries the wounds from such atrocities which require healing to raise vibration. Love, compassion, and empathy sprout in higher frequencies while fear, shame, and self-doubt sprout in lower ones. This is not a hierarchical distinction; it is a qualitative one. I think of higher frequency as nutrient-rich soil and lower frequency as soil that lacks nutrients.

WORKING WITHIN THE PATRIARCHY

The contemporary church struggles with the same challenge highlighted in the gospel today. Judging the Pharisees and Sadducees participation in his baptism as insincere, John says to them, "You brood of vipers! Who warned you to flee from the coming wrath?" (3:7). If baptism is about repentance of sins, how do we identify sincere repentance? Can infants sincerely repent? If repentance is not something that we do, but something stirred within us as we are baptized, how is our sincerity a factor?

My chaplaincy experience involved many baptismal questions. I routinely ran into second births where the parents were not married when their first child was born. They subsequently married before the second child arrived. The conversations went something like this:

"We would like to have our children baptized, but the Catholic Church will not do it because we had a child out of wedlock. Can you do it?"

"It depends on what you are looking for. If you want documentation of the baptism for church records and eventual confirmation, you will want the baptism to take place in a church. If it is for your personal desire, anyone can baptize."

"We would like it in a church but feel badly about how we were treated. Would your church baptize both children?

"Yes, but you would need to meet with the church pastor and attend services."

On several occasions, the couple requested that I set up a meeting, and I would meet with the local ELCA pastor to do so. These were always frustrating meetings. The pastor wanted the couple to become members before baptizing the children to demonstrate their sincerity which always felt like conditional love to the parents. Conditions alienated them from the church in the first place.

I never understood baptism and/or grace as something anyone had to earn. I did not understand the cakes that read, "Welcome to God's family." During the rite of baptism, I described baptism as an affirmation of God's love instead. The perspective of unworthiness stems from the theology of original sin—that there is something in human nature that is innately sinful. The idea of innate sinfulness, despite anything that we think, say, or do helps breed guilt and shame.

A READING FROM *THE GOSPEL OF MARY*: PAGES 7-8

While Peter said to him: "Since you've explained everything to us, tell us one more thing. What's the sin of the world?"

The Savior (most translations use the word "Teacher" instead), "Sin doesn't exist, but you're the ones who make sin when you act in accordance with the nature of adultery, which is called 'sin.'"

walk within

NOTES

CONTEMPLATING *THE GOSPEL OF MARY*

The Gospel of Mary offers an alternative understanding of sin. When Peter asks Jesus, "What's the sin of the world?" Jesus replies, "Sin doesn't exist." We can almost hear a pin drop. How can we possibly believe that sin doesn't exist? "Just look around," we think to ourselves. Watch the news. "Impossible," we may think. But as we listen, we hear Jesus continue, " . . . but you're the ones who make sin when you act in accordance with the nature of adultery, which is called sin." American culture most often limits its understanding of the word "adultery" to fornication. The Greek carries a broader understanding meaning "to alter" like something being adulterated. If our nature is corrupted, it cannot be corrupt initially. No original sin exists in *The Gospel of Mary*. The question becomes, what alters our nature?

Handing responsibility for our lives to others rather than assuming responsibility for ourselves alters our nature. Seeking to escape our responsibility by numbing ourselves, denying our purposes, comparing ourselves with others, seeking perfection rather than learning from imperfections, hiding our authenticity, refusing to use our voices, shaming ourselves and others alter our nature to such a degree that we forget what our nature is. Numb and atrophied our hearts paralyze us. The paralysis lowers our vibrations until we fall asleep and become nothing more than cogs in an assembly line of life.

WHAT IF?

What if nothing is sinful and there are no sinners? What if every experience on earth is a learning opportunity? When do we learn best? Do we learn best when we feel bad about ourselves and feel ashamed? Fear and shame only yield momentary obedience, perpetuating agreements according to outside influences. But when we see potential for growth and healing, we generalize our applications to other situations. We are more willing to risk making mistakes to develop and grow. I recently read an article about the book *Raising an Entrepreneur*. To write the book, author Margot Machol Bisnow interviewed 70 parents who had raised highly successful adults who are resilient, hard-working initiators who bring ideas to life. The parents held four rules of parenting in common: give children extreme independence, actively nurture compassion, welcome failure early and often, and let go of control and lead by following. What if these were the ways that we viewed God/Divine/Source/Beloved/Wisdom/Wholeness/Creator/Spirit/Energy/(Other)_____ guiding all of us?

POST-READING INTEGRATIONS

1. What is your understanding of sin?

2. Describe an experience that taught you compassion.

3. Describe a time that you learned something through failure or by making a mistake. What did you learn?

4. When do you let go of control and lead by following?

CHAPTER 7

Orthodoxy and Heresy– Year A: Advent Week III

PRE-READING REFLECTIONS

1. What is your definition of Orthodoxy? How did you come to this understanding?

2. What is your definition of Heresy? How did you come to this understanding?

3. How do Orthodoxy and Heresy integrate for you?

A FIRST TESTAMENT READING FROM ISAIAH 35: 1-10

35 ¹ The desert and the parched land will be glad;
   the wilderness will rejoice and blossom.
Like the crocus, ² it will burst into bloom;
   it will rejoice greatly and shout for joy.
The glory of Lebanon will be given to it,
   the splendor of Carmel and Sharon;
they will see the glory of the Lord,
   the splendor of our God.
³ Strengthen the feeble hands,
   steady the knees that give way;
⁴ say to those with fearful hearts,
   "Be strong, do not fear;
your God will come,
   he will come with vengeance;
with divine retribution
   he will come to save you."
⁵ Then will the eyes of the blind be opened
   and the ears of the deaf unstopped.
⁶ Then will the lame leap like a deer,
   and the mute tongue shout for joy.
Water will gush forth in the wilderness
   and streams in the desert.
⁷ The burning sand will become a pool,
   the thirsty ground bubbling springs.
In the haunts where jackals once lay,
   grass and reeds and papyrus will grow.
Gladness and joy will overtake them,
   and sorrow and sighing will flee away.
⁸ And a highway will be there;
it will be called the Way of Holiness;
   it will be for those who walk on that Way.
The unclean will not journey on it;
   wicked fools will not go about on it.

⁹ No lion will be there,
   nor any ravenous beast;
   they will not be found there.
But only the redeemed will walk there,
¹⁰   and those the Lord has rescued will return.
They will enter Zion with singing;
   everlasting joy will crown their heads.
Gladness and joy will overtake them,
   and sorrow and sighing will flee away.

NOTES

A READING FROM PSALM 146: 5-10

⁵ Blessed are those whose help is the God of Jacob,
   whose hope is in the Lord their God.
⁶ He is the Maker of heaven and earth,
   the sea, and everything in them—
   he remains faithful forever.
⁷ He upholds the cause of the oppressed
   and gives food to the hungry.
The Lord sets prisoners free,
⁸   the Lord gives sight to the blind,
the Lord lifts up those who are bowed down,
   the Lord loves the righteous.
⁹ The Lord watches over the foreigner
   and sustains the fatherless and the widow,
   but he frustrates the ways of the wicked.
¹⁰ The Lord reigns forever,
   your God, O Zion, for all generations.

Orthodoxy and Heresy—Year A: Advent Week III

NOTES

A SECOND TESTAMENT READING FROM JAMES 5: 7-10

⁷ Be patient, then, brothers and sisters, until the Lord's coming. See how the farmer waits for the land to yield its valuable crop, patiently waiting for the autumn and spring rains. ⁸ You too, be patient and stand firm, because the Lord's coming is near. ⁹ Don't grumble against one another, brothers and sisters, or you will be judged. The Judge is standing at the door!
¹⁰ Brothers and sisters, as an example of patience in the face of suffering, take the prophets who spoke in the name of the Lord.

Orthodoxy and Heresy–Year A: Advent Week III

NOTES

A READING FROM MATTHEW 11: 2-11 (NIV)

² When John, who was in prison, heard about the deeds of the Messiah, he sent his disciples³ to ask him, "Are you the one who is to come, or should we expect someone else?"
⁴ Jesus replied, "Go back and report to John what you hear and see: ⁵ The blind receive sight, the lame walk, those who have leprosy[a] are cleansed, the deaf hear, the dead are raised, and the good news is proclaimed to the poor. ⁶ Blessed is anyone who does not stumble on account of me."
⁷ As John's disciples were leaving, Jesus began to speak to the crowd about John: "What did you go out into the wilderness to see? A reed swayed by the wind? ⁸ If not, what did you go out to see? A man dressed in fine clothes? No, those who wear fine clothes are in kings' palaces. ⁹ Then what did you go out to see? A prophet? Yes, I tell you, and more than a prophet. ¹⁰ This is the one about whom it is written:
"'I will send my messenger ahead of you,
    who will prepare your way before you.'[b]
¹¹ Truly I tell you, among those born of women there has not risen anyone greater than John the Baptist; yet whoever is least in the kingdom of heaven is greater than he.

NOTES

A READING FROM MATTHEW 11: 2-11 (MSG)

²⁻³ John, meanwhile, had been locked up in prison. When he got wind of what Jesus was doing, he sent his own disciples to ask, "Are you the One we've been expecting, or are we still waiting?"

⁴⁻⁶ Jesus told them, "Go back and tell John what's going on:
The blind see,
The lame walk,
Lepers are cleansed,
The deaf hear,
The dead are raised,
The wretched of the earth learn that God is on their side.
"Is this what you were expecting? Then count yourselves most blessed!"

⁷⁻¹⁰ When John's disciples left to report, Jesus started talking to the crowd about John. "What did you expect when you went out to see him in the wild? A weekend camper? Hardly. What then? A sheik in silk pajamas? Not in the wilderness, not by a long shot. What then? A prophet? That's right, a prophet! Probably the best prophet you'll ever hear. He is the prophet that Malachi announced when he wrote, 'I'm sending my prophet ahead of you, to make the road smooth for you.'

¹¹ "Let me tell you what's going on here: No one in history surpasses John the Baptizer; but in the kingdom he prepared you for, the lowliest person is ahead of him.

Orthodoxy and Heresy-Year A: Advent Week III

NOTES

CONTEMPLATING *THE GOSPEL OF MATTHEW* 11: 2-11

As you will see, this text and lesson funnel into the issues of orthodoxy and heresy and how they foster duality in human lives throughout Christian history. The examples shared focus on women and the loss of the Divine Feminine through patriarchal leadership. This greatly contributes to the loss of options in an orthodoxy and heresy divided world.

Since John the Baptist first asked if "Jesus is the one to come" (v. 3), the question continued to echo throughout history in a variety of contexts. John is asking if Jesus is the Messiah King who will overthrow the government as prophesied in the First Testament. This is significant because there are others claiming to be, or being identified as, the Messiah at the same time. The Messianic movement also entailed purging the Israelites of gentiles. The immediate years following the story of Jesus' resurrection involved a variety of answers to John's question. Paul worked to integrate Jesus as the prophesied First Testament Messiah and suggested Jesus as the God of a variety of gentile communities who answered John's question differently.

In this reading Jesus ends his response to John's question with these words, "Blessed is anyone who does not stumble on account of me" (v. 6). At first glance, it seems that Jesus blesses those who do not stumble because Jesus helps keep them from stumbling. A closer look, taken thousands of years later, raises the question of all who have stumbled *on account* of Jesus. This is not how we typically think about Jesus. But, given thousands of years of Christian history, "stumbling on account of Jesus" can make great sense. Attempting to twist the words of Jesus to suit needs and rationalizing actions in Jesus' name when this was not possible, religious leaders stumbled, tortured, and murdered in his name. A brief review of The destruction of the Alexandrian Library, The Crusades, and Inquisitions exemplify this. It also documents the patriarchy's best attempts to marginalize and destroy women as representatives of the Divine Feminine.

ANCIENT WORLD

The Library of Alexandria, one of the largest and most significant libraries of the ancient world, housed a variety of sacred writings that grew as a result of the hospitality it showed to spiritual leaders. Constantine's desire for a canon birthed formalization of heresies concerning Jesus' identity. He legalized Christianity through the Edict of Milan in 313 CE and began calling for councils to create a canon in 325 CE. His command to destroy all other writings drove mothers and fathers to write and copy the newly decreed heretical works into the desert. The act of evaluating teachings and actions as orthodox or heretical expanded when Christianity became the state religion of the Roman empire under Emperor Theodosius with the Edict of Thessalonica in 380 CE.

Subsequently, the earth and the Divine Feminine was further undermined. For example, Hypatia, a pagan mathematician, philosopher, and astronomer finding the Divine in science, refused to convert to Christianity. As the daughter of Theon, the librarian of the Library of Alexandria, she was well educated and known for her wise counsel. At the same time, many sacred writings held by the library were considered heretical and destroyed at Archbishop Cyril's direction. View the film, *Agora* for a reasonably accurate depiction of these events. The first time that I watched it, I couldn't believe the events were true. After doing some research, I discovered the reality was worse than the film depicted.

The parabalani, a volunteer militia of monks serving as henchmen to the archbishop, understood nothing of Hypatia's philosophy and viewed her as a pagan heretic. They pulled the elder from her chariot as she rode through the city and dragged her to a temple. There they stripped her naked, skinned her with jagged pieces of oyster shells, pulled her limbs from her body and paraded them through the streets. Finally, they burned them in a mockery of pagan sacrifice. Hypatia's death marked the end of paganism and the triumph of Christianity. From this point, Christianity spread via a "convert or die" enforcement of the canon and the law. Religion romanticizes the spread of Christianity rather than acknowledging the brutality involved.

CRUSADES

Classical antiquity considered Jerusalem the center of the world—the place where God resided. Jews viewed Jerusalem as the holiest city in Judaism and the ancestral and spiritual homeland of the Jewish people since the 10th century BCE. Muslims consider Jerusalem a site of key events in the life of Jesus and other important figures. It's also the spot where, according to traditional interpretations of the Koran and other texts, the prophet Muhammad ascended to heaven. For Christians, Jesus preached, died, and rose from the dead in Jerusalem. Many also see the city as central to the second coming of Jesus. During the Crusades, all three of these faith traditions laid claim to Jerusalem and the surrounding lands.

The Crusades involved a series of wars for control of Jerusalem and other gates to the city. The controversial death estimates for the Crusades range from one million to nine million people from approximately 1095-1291 CE. Control of Jerusalem exchanged hands from the Byzantine Empire to Christians. Thereafter, Jerusalem exchanged hands between Muslims and Christians by occupation, political alliances, and marriages. Christians finally lost Jerusalem with the defeat at Acre in 1291.

Women played significant roles in the first two crusades. Research highlights how women worked to advance their ideals, to minimize bloodshed and to free themselves from church limitations. The following women whose names and actions survived through history demonstrate their sovereignty.

Anna Comnea (1083-1153) attempted a coup to put her husband on the Byzantine throne rather than her brother. When it failed, she wrote her family history depicting "the knights of the first crusades not as saviors but as looters who turned greedy eyes to the gold, enamel, and artwork of Byzantium." [12]

Eleanor of Aquitaine (1120-1204) led 300 of her women dressed as amazons and a thousand of her knights in the armies of the Second Crusade. She insisted on taking part in strategy sessions and sided with her uncle, Raymond of Antioch, instead of her husband, Louis VII of France, on the question of whether to attack Jerusalem. Louis settled the argument by insisting that she accompany him to Jerusalem. The King and Queen of France went home on separate ships. When back in Europe, after giving birth to a daughter, Eleanor insisted on a divorce and married Henry II of England.

During the Second Crusade, the Church officially discouraged women rulers from taking vows of crusading. Western women did continue to accompany men to the wars, as the sister and wife of Richard the Lion-Hearted did in the Third Crusade, but they went along in a private capacity. The only women that the Church officially approved for part of the Crusaders army was the washerwomen. They played a vital role in washing clothes to prevent the spread of lice, and they were usually considered too old to be a temptation for men.

The Christian church's official discouragement did not dissuade the women who wanted to fight from participating. During the third crusade, Shagrat al-Durr (d. 1259) wife of the Egyptian sultan, organized the defense of the realm during her husband's illness, became sultan due to the support of the army upon his death, and defeated The King of France, Louis IX, at Damietta.

The paladins, who created the Frankish Kingdoms of the East after the First Crusade, intermarried with the women of the East, particularly Armenian Christians. One of the children of these unions was Melisende, the daughter of Baldwin II, who married Morphia while Count of Edessa. Melisende (1105-1160), Queen of Jerusalem, ruled the Frankish Kingdom of Jerusalem jointly with her husband or son while vying with them for supreme power. [13]

The experience of women such as Anna, Eleanor, Shagrat, and Melisende proves that women were capable of seizing power as opportunities arose. All these women garnered a strong patriarchal response and found it easier to exercise power through a husband or son. Having to function in this manner led to its own issues of heresy and orthodoxy whenever women were allowed to fight but not allowed to grow and prosper.

THE CRUSADE AGAINST THE CATHARS

While control of holy lands clearly prompted Crusades, beliefs surrounding heresy and orthodoxy also played a role in the desires to control them. All the groups involved didn't want organizations with faith traditions inconsistent with their own controlling land that they viewed as holy. While the Albigensian Crusade primarily involved heretical accusations, church and civil authorities used middle eastern crusading strategies to navigate them.

Cathars lived simple, non-violent lives in France. They did not acknowledge the First Testament of the bible. Focusing upon the Second Testament, they primarily followed the Gospel of John. Prefects served as spiritual teachers and leaders. Women also served as prefects. Cathars saw no reason to marginalize women. They held a belief in what we might refer to as reincarnation. Anyone may be a woman or man in past or future lives, so it did not make sense to marginalize anyone. After initiation Prefects became vegetarians while Cathars could eat anything. Non-Prefect Cathars received the same initiation as they prepared to transition from the material world into the spiritual world through death.

The catholic church deemed all these practices heretical. While their crusade against the Cathars immediately experienced some success in the North of France due to the support of civil authorities, it ultimately caused Cathars to migrate south. Southern authorities did not follow the north's practice of executing anyone that the church identified as a heretic. Consequently, Catharism grew in Southern France, particularly among the nobility and the common people.

Royal women marginalized by the church found a place to practice equality in Cathar communities.

Several events culminate in what was previously called the Albigensian Crusade because it took place near Albi. Highly populated by Cathars, Albi served as a central location of the Cathar region and housed the Cathar equivalent of Bishops. Unlike the groups willing to fight in the middle eastern crusades, the Cathars were pacifists with no desire nor resources to shed the blood of those who thought differently than they did.

This makes what happened more alarming. From 1209 to 1215 the Crusaders experienced great success due in part to Pope Innocent III's offer of Cathar lands to any French noble willing to fight against them. Cathars and their supporters regained lands through revolts 1216-1225. French royals capitalized on the situation by joining the crusade as a means of annexing more land for France. A series of castle sieges ended the military aspects of the Crusade, and it informally transitioned to an Inquisition with approximately 80,000 Cathars burned for Heresy on April 12, 1229. In 1234 Pope Gregory IX formally established an Inquisition and on March 16, 1244, 200 Cathar prefects died at the stake. Loss of leadership effectively drove Catharism underground.

Burning was an especially heinous way for Cathars to die. They believed that the body must be buried to resurrect. In most cases there was nothing left to bury. Historians estimate that 200,000 to one million died throughout this campaign. Not all of them were Cathars. Out of sheer frustration, "the catholic church decided to burn anyone who was in the way and to let God sort them out."[14]

ADDITIONAL INQUISITIONS

While the Cathar Crusade transitioned to an Inquisition that moved from acquisition of land to accusations of heresy, other inquisitions simply began as hunts for heretics. The Divine Feminine embodied by Joan of Arc at age 19 was tortured and burned at the stake on

May 30, 1431. Labeled a heretic, fraud, sorceress and crossdresser, she refused to recant the visions that she experienced as communication with God.

The Spanish Inquisition helped solidify the monarchy as the Spanish Kingdom expanded from 1478-1834. During the Spanish Inquisition, Jews and Muslims faced persecution and pressure to convert to Christianity. Common women tried by the Spanish Inquisition were accused of Judaizing, of observing Jewish law and rites, and of believing that salvation would be attained in this manner. The Church viewed these actions as heretical because those being judged were baptized Catholics and not Jews. Historians estimate 30,000 to millions of lives lost during this time.

What I call an "inquisition mindset" accompanied colonization. Indigenous peoples around the world who honored the land and the spirit within all things were declared heretics. The label of "heretic" rationalized enslavement, theft of lands, persecution and genocide in various forms. From the middle passage to Indian Boarding Schools the evidence is overwhelming. Most significant is the fact that the catholic church maintains an open Inquisition office today. Scholars agree that approximately 56 million lives were lost in this process.

Until the 14th century, wichas or wise women were the only healers available to commoners. They also served nobles and others seeking healing. It was not until 1390 that "witchcraft" was declared a crime for the first time in France. Other countries followed a similar path between the 14th and 18th centuries. While the church acknowledges hundreds of thousands lost in the witch hunts that followed, recent research suggests 8-9 million people lost. These losses grew as women labeled as heretics fled to their homes. There the church burned all the inhabitants of their towns or villages and accessed the land. A clear pattern between acquiring land, targeting heretics and legalizing murder quickly emerges when we take time to examine history. Unknown by many, the loss of life continued through the Reformation.

WARS OF REFORMATION

Five million people died in the Reformation wars that ensued between 1517 and 1618. Ultimately, the wars ended with the agreement that each nation could choose its own religion. Orthodoxy and heresy continued to be identified nation-by-nation according to the religions they chose. Patriarchy "allowed" women to learn to read. This enabled reading the bible, writing in support of men's efforts, and expanding limitations through men. Despite their education and their efforts to support the Reformation, all of these women continued to endure ridicule and abuse. These are just a few of the women now being acknowledged for their unique contributions.

Margarete de Navarre (1492-1549) was the sister of King Frances of France. She received the same education as her brother. One of her poems, entitled "Mirror of the Sinful Soul," described a personal relationship with Jesus as a father-brother. "Her work caused such an uproar among the priests and bishops in France that they recommended she be sewed into a sack and thrown into the river."[15] She influenced the Reformation in England through the translation of her poem which was condemned as heretical by the Catholic Church. She worked to protect those who would otherwise have been arrested and executed as heretics.

Marie Dentiere (1495-1561): is the only woman whose name appears on the Reformation Wall monument in Geneva. She rejected the patriarchal view that women were incapable of understanding, much less preaching scripture and cited female figures from the Bible as support for her claims. She encouraged Marguerite de Navarre to banish the Catholic clergy from France. Heavily involved in education, she started a girl's school and wrote a French grammar book.

Argula von Grumbach (1592 -1554) tapped into the vast amount of scripture that she had memorized to write an elegant letter defending a young Lutheran teacher at the University of Ingolstadt who was arrested for heresy. Using over 80 scripture references in her letter, she promoted the Word of God above the word of the pope, the Kaiser, and Aristotle. This letter was published as a booklet and became a bestseller. "She was shunned by her in laws, faced nobles, kings, and princes, and a husband who had been advised to either strangle her, or at least disable her, so she couldn't write. Regularly denounced as a whore and shunned by many of her family and friends, she continued writing, corresponding with Luther, and even traveling alone to preach on the new teachings until her death from unknown causes in 1564." [16]

While these women did not fight on the literal battlefield, their intelligence and writing skills fueled the movement. Undeterred by outside critics, they continued their efforts even when the men who initially provided protection went to war or died of other causes. They saw their freedom at stake in a movement to reform the catholic church that would not honor their gifts. Once the wars ended, many of the protestant denominations also denied the gifts of women whose words had persuaded so many to support their cause. The most progressive Lutheran church has only been ordaining women for 50 years. Many still do not ordain them.

> **A READING FROM *THE GOSPEL OF MARY*: PAGE 17**
>
> In response Peter spoke out with the same concerns. He asked them concerning the Savior: "He didn't speak with a woman without our knowledge and not publicly with us, did he? Will we turn around and all listen to her? Did he prefer her to us?"

Orthodoxy and Heresy-Year A: Advent Week III

NOTES

CONTEMPLATING *THE GOSPEL OF MARY*

Peter's questions in *The Gospel of Mary*, "Must we change our customs, and listen to this woman? Did he really choose her, and prefer her to us?" indicate that Jesus entered a mysoginistic world. It confounds me that religious leaders continue to stumble and use the bible to suggest that Jesus counted women as somehow inferior and less capable. Jesus didn't do this, but it appears some people around him did.

According to the church's own biblical sources, women followed, supported, and financed Jesus' ministry. They stood at the foot of the cross, anointed his lifeless body, and testified to his resurrection. Does any of this matter? Can it matter if we continue to stumble on account of what Jesus and his message have come to mean? Can it matter if we think he came so that we may use his name to make any one of us superior to another? The stories of Jesus show him helping the downtrodden, the discarded, the diminished, and the marginalized to demonstrate that there is no superiority.

However, there is leadership. According to *The Gospel of Mary*, Jesus equipped Mary to lead the disciples once he was gone. He saw in her the humility and the trust to raise their spirits and to inspire them to share Jesus' message of Love rather than to seek status. Perhaps he was naïve in the way we feel naïve when things do not go as we planned. Or maybe the rediscovery of *The Gospel of Mary* near the end of WWII was another chance to understand and to avoid stumbling on account of Jesus, just as the world we live in today is yet another.

WHAT IF?

In today's reading from Matthew, Jesus' response to John's question, "Are you the one who is to come, or should we expect someone else?" does not match the First Testament description of a king nor most of the actions taken in Jesus' name following his life and death. Jesus answers, "Go back and report to John what you hear and see: The blind receive sight, the lame walk, those who have leprosy are cleansed, the deaf hear, the dead are raised, and the good news is proclaimed to the poor. Most of the healings in Matthew end with Jesus affirming that those healed play a co-creative role in their healing. What if Jesus is calling our attention to our own roles in healing the stories in our heads, the feelings in our hearts, the actions we take in anyone's name but our own, the choices by which we live, and the systems with which we maintain our relationships?

POST-CONTEMPLATION INTEGRATIONS

1. Have you stumbled on account of Jesus? If so, describe the experience.

2. How do you define healing?

3. How are you a co-creator?

CHAPTER 8

Preparing the Way for Mary– Year A: Advent Week IV

PRE-READING REFLECTIONS

1. What I understand about Joseph, Jesus' father, and how I came to learn it:

2. Jesus' teachings that are important to me and how I learned them:

Jesus' Teaching . . .	How I learned it . . .

3. What I understand about Mary Magdalene and how I came to understand these things:

What I understand about Mary Magdalene . . .	How I came to understand this . . .

A FIRST TESTAMENT READING FROM ISAIAH 7: 10-16

[10] Again the Lord spoke to Ahaz, [11] "Ask the Lord your God for a sign, whether in the deepest depths or in the highest heights."
[12] But Ahaz said, "I will not ask; I will not put the Lord to the test."
[13] Then Isaiah said, "Hear now, you house of David! Is it not enough to try the patience of humans? Will you try the patience of my God also? [14] Therefore the Lord himself will give you[a] a sign: The virgin[b] will conceive and give birth to a son, and[c] will call him Immanuel.[d] [15] He will be eating curds and honey when he knows enough to reject the wrong and choose the right, [16] for before the boy knows enough to reject the wrong and choose the right, the land of the two kings you dread will be laid waste.

NOTES

A READING FROM PSALM 80: 1-7 and 17-19

¹ Hear us, Shepherd of Israel,
  you who lead Joseph like a flock.
You who sit enthroned between the cherubim,
  shine forth ² before Ephraim, Benjamin and Manasseh.
Awaken your might;
  come and save us.
³ Restore us, O God;
  make your face shine on us,
  that we may be saved.
⁴ How long, Lord God Almighty,
  will your anger smolder
  against the prayers of your people?
⁵ You have fed them with the bread of tears;
  you have made them drink tears by the bowlful.
⁶ You have made us an object of derision[b] to our neighbors,
  and our enemies mock us.
⁷ Restore us, God Almighty;
  make your face shine on us,
  that we may be saved.

¹⁷ Let your hand rest on the man at your right hand,
  the son of man you have raised up for yourself.
¹⁸ Then we will not turn away from you;
  revive us, and we will call on your name.
¹⁹ Restore us, Lord God Almighty;
  make your face shine on us,
  that we may be saved.

NOTES

A SECOND TESTAMENT READING FROM PAUL'S LETTER TO THE ROMANS 1: 1-7

¹ Paul, a servant of Christ Jesus, called to be an apostle and set apart for the gospel of God— ² the gospel he promised beforehand through his prophets in the Holy Scriptures ³ regarding his Son, who as to his earthly life[a] was a descendant of David, ⁴ and who through the Spirit of holiness was appointed the Son of God in power[b] by his resurrection from the dead: Jesus Christ our Lord. ⁵ Through him we received grace and apostleship to call all the Gentiles to the obedience that comes from[c] faith for his name's sake. ⁶ And you also are among those Gentiles who are called to belong to Jesus Christ.

⁷ To all in Rome who are loved by God and called to be his holy people:

Grace and peace to you from God our Father and from the Lord Jesus Christ.

NOTES

A READING FROM MATTHEW 1: 18-25 (NIV)

[18] This is how the birth of Jesus the Messiah came about[a]: His mother Mary was pledged to be married to Joseph, but before they came together, she was found to be pregnant through the Holy Spirit. [19] Because Joseph her husband was faithful to the law, and yet[b] did not want to expose her to public disgrace, he had in mind to divorce her quietly.
[20] But after he had considered this, an angel of the Lord appeared to him in a dream and said, "Joseph son of David, do not be afraid to take Mary home as your wife, because what is conceived in her is from the Holy Spirit. [21] She will give birth to a son, and you are to give him the name Jesus,[c] because he will save his people from their sins."
[22] All this took place to fulfill what the Lord had said through the prophet: [23] "The virgin will conceive and give birth to a son, and they will call him Immanuel"[d] (which means "God with us").
[24] When Joseph woke up, he did what the angel of the Lord had commanded him and took Mary home as his wife. [25] But he did not consummate their marriage until she gave birth to a son. And he gave him the name Jesus.

NOTES

A READING FROM *THE GOSPEL OF MATTHEW* 1: 18-25 (MSG)

¹⁸⁻¹⁹ The birth of Jesus took place like this. His mother, Mary, was engaged to be married to Joseph. Before they enjoyed their wedding night, Joseph discovered she was pregnant. (It was by the Holy Spirit, but he didn't know that.) Joseph, chagrined but noble, determined to take care of things quietly so Mary would not be disgraced.

²⁰⁻²³ While he was trying to figure a way out, he had a dream. God's angel spoke in the dream: "Joseph, son of David, don't hesitate to get married. Mary's pregnancy is Spirit-conceived. God's Holy Spirit has made her pregnant. She will bring a son to birth, and when she does, you, Joseph, will name him Jesus—'God saves'—because he will save his people from their sins." This would bring the prophet's embryonic revelation to full term:

Watch for this—a virgin will get pregnant and bear a son; They will name him Immanuel (Hebrew for "God is with us").

²⁴⁻²⁵ Then Joseph woke up. He did exactly what God's angel commanded in the dream: He married Mary. But he did not consummate the marriage until she had the baby. He named the baby Jesus.

Preparing the Way for Mary–Year A: Advent Week IVI

NOTES

CONTEMPLATING *THE GOSPEL OF MATTHEW*

I remember sitting in the gymnasium during an all-school liturgy while teaching at a Jesuit high school. A priest who was a friend of mine preached the homily for the Feast of The Immaculate Conception. As a Lutheran, it was the first time I heard the Immaculate Conception described as Mary being sinless—without original sin. I leaned over the bleachers where the faculty sat during the service expecting to see surprise on other faculty members' faces. None greeted me. Apparently, I was the only one in the room who thought the Immaculate Conception was about a virgin birth rendering Jesus free of sin rather than about Mary being free from sin.

After the service, I searched for my friend and caught up with him in the hall.

"Can I ask you a question, Terry?"

"Sure," he replied, turning around to greet me.

"If Mary is perfect, why did we need Jesus?"

With a stunned look on his face, all he said was my name drawn out slowly, "C r y s t a l." It was as if even thinking or asking any question that would impact the church's teachings ought to be reconsidered before being uttered.

"And, where does it say Mary was perfect in the bible?" I responded, undeterred. It just never made sense to me that a perfect god, a divine being, or a state of consciousness would require us to accept things that did not make sense somehow—intellectually, metaphorically, intuitively, or any other kind of knowing that inspires resonance. I could not accept that faith, by definition, ought to render us mindless and put us to sleep.

"It's not in the bible, it's tradition!" he said, turning on his heels to continue walking down the hall and to avoid further conversation.

Tradition surrounds Joseph as there is little historical information about him. Canonically, he first appears in our reading today. He appears a second time when inspired to flee to Egypt to protect his family and a third when he is told to return to Galilee. We see him for the last time when Jesus is 12 years old and found in the temple teaching after his parents spent a day frantically searching for him. The bible does not mention Joseph after this event. Biblical scholars hypothesize that Joseph died before Jesus' ministry began. While Jesus' mother, Mary, witnesses his first miracle during the wedding at Cana and stands at the foot of the cross, Joseph is not mentioned as attending either event. Scholars also suggest that Jesus' words announcing that John shall care for his mother after he dies imply that Joseph is dead.

The Joseph described in the gospels comes from the line of Nathan traced back to Abraham. Abiding by the inspiration of his dreams, he protects his family despite the risk of social gossip. Then he simply disappears from the canon.

THE GOSPEL OF MARY: PAGE 18

Then Mary wept and said to Peter,
"My brother Peter, what are you thinking?
Do you really think that I thought this up by myself in my heart, or that I am lying about the Savior?"

In response Levi said to Peter, "Peter, you've always been angry. Now I see you debating with this woman like the adversaries. But if the Savior made her worthy, who are you then to reject her?"

Preparing the Way for Mary—Year A: Advent Week IV

NOTES

CONTEMPLATING *THE GOSPEL OF MARY:* PAGE 18

After sharing what Peter asks of her, Peter rebukes and attempts to dismiss Mary. Can we imagine what it was like to vulnerably honor Peter's request and describe the deepest experience one shared with Jesus only to have it angrily dismissed? I don't think this is very difficult for most women to imagine. Women are unilaterally dismissed throughout the world. So, what is more surprising here? That the Teacher affirms Mary's wisdom or that Peter cannot understand because said wisdom comes from a woman? In the time Jesus lived, the status of a woman was determined by a man—her father, her betrothed, her husband or her son when widowed. Without these connections, risk of poverty and food scarcity increased.

Yet, women left their assigned roles to follow Jesus. Some financed his ministry and participated in ways we attribute to deaconesses today. They weren't just supporting Jesus with their finances. They followed him as disciples and ministered alongside him. The author of Luke specifically names Mary Magdalene and Joanna, the wife of Chuza (also a follower and royal official). It is not only *The Gospel of Mary* that asserts that Mary learned and shared with Jesus, but also another canonical gospel. This puts us at a point of choice. Do we, like Peter, the Council Fathers, and religions of the Christian church, dismiss Mary's voice? Or do we embrace it, perhaps even dare to embody it, as we awaken?

Scholars believe Levi, a Jewish tax collector, becomes known by the Christian name, Matthew, when he replaces Judas as a disciple. This provides an interesting bridge between today's readings from the gospel of Matthew and *The Gospel of Mary*. We do not know who wrote any of the gospels in the sense of historical documentation. Within the gospels themselves, scholars suggest that the gospel of Matthew for Year A of The Revised Common Lectionary was written by the tax collector known as Levi who replaced Judas and changed his name to Matthew. It is interesting to imagine one of the gospel writers, themselves, affirming Mary's leadership as Levi does when he says, "Peter, you've always been angry. Now I see you debating with this woman like the adversaries. But if the Savior made her worthy, who are you then to reject her?"

The question, "Who are you then to reject her?" echoes through both of today's readings. Joseph intends to reject Jesus' mother, Mary by breaking off the engagement quietly without disgracing her when he learns that she is pregnant. An angel appears in his dream to tell him not to follow his plan. Instead, Joseph is to remain with her given divine intent. In the same way, Levi reminds Peter not to dismiss Mary Magdalene's teachings or the Teacher's divine intent. Rather than disgracing Mary as their adversaries disgrace and dismiss women, Levi suggests that they live and teach as Mary guides them.

WHAT IF?

What if Jesus came to prepare the way for Mary? What if he came to elevate the status of women—especially the status of Mary Magdalene? What if the meaning of Jesus' life does not involve his or his mother's perfection, but rather a way of being instead? A way of being understood by those with ears to hear and eyes to see. What if the apostle with those eyes and ears at that point in time was Mary Magdalene?

Just who did lead the Way after Jesus? Bible history asserts that James, the brother of Jesus, received a vision of Jesus and led the way in Jerusalem. We know that Paul traveled to lead the way in the gentile world by the letters he wrote to the communities that he visited. Peter became the rock on which the catholic church rests. What if Mary led the way through Egypt and Provence, France as the history in France so clearly suggests?

Do we need to look any further than the reversal of Roe v. Wade to understand the trouble Peter had with this? To understand the misogyny that dismisses, disgraces, and disregards the voices of women? To understand the self-hatred bred by such misogyny that causes women to vote against women making choices about their own bodies like the women luring young girls into sex trafficking?

I recently heard Don Miquel Ruiz Jr. recall one of his father's teachings. He recalled his father saying that there is no right or wrong choice (in and of itself). When we choose correctly for our lives, we stay the course. When we choose incorrectly for ourselves, we course correct. The challenge his father identified was that when our egos will not allow us to course correct, we continue in a direction that is inauthentic to our lives. What if Mary Magdalene's leadership and teachings were a course correction for the men who did not yet have ears to hear or eyes to see?

POST-READING INTEGRATIONS

1. Describe a time when you had ears to hear and eyes to see:
2. How do you know when your consciousness has fallen asleep?

Preparing the Way for Mary–Year A: Advent Week IVI

3. What wakes your consciousness up?

CHAPTER 9

Womb Awakening-Year A: Christmas/Solstice

PRE-READING REFLECTIONS

1. How I celebrate Solstice/Christmas/(Other) _____:

2. My understanding of Jesus' birth and how I learned it:

3. Advent means "coming." However we celebrate the season, Christmas/Solstice involves arrival. What is arriving for you this season?

A FIRST TESTAMENT READING FROM ISAIAH 52: 7-10

⁷ How beautiful on the mountains
   are the feet of those who bring good news,
who proclaim peace,
   who bring good tidings,
   who proclaim salvation,
who say to Zion,
   "Your God reigns!"
⁸ Listen! Your watchmen lift up their voices;
   together they shout for joy.
When the Lord returns to Zion,
   they will see it with their own eyes.
⁹ Burst into songs of joy together,
   you ruins of Jerusalem,
for the Lord has comforted his people,
   he has redeemed Jerusalem.
¹⁰ The Lord will lay bare his holy arm
   in the sight of all the nations,
and all the ends of the earth will see
   the salvation of our God.

NOTES

A READING FROM PSALM 98: 1-9

¹ Sing to the Lord a new song,
  for he has done marvelous things;
his right hand and his holy arm
  have worked salvation for him.
² The Lord has made his salvation known
  and revealed his righteousness to the nations.
³ He has remembered his love
  and his faithfulness to Israel;
all the ends of the earth have seen
  the salvation of our God.
⁴ Shout for joy to the Lord, all the earth,
  burst into jubilant song with music;
⁵ make music to the Lord with the harp,
  with the harp and the sound of singing,
⁶ with trumpets and the blast of the ram's horn—
  shout for joy before the Lord, the King.
⁷ Let the sea resound, and everything in it,
  the world, and all who live in it.
⁸ Let the rivers clap their hands,
  let the mountains sing together for joy;
⁹ let them sing before the Lord,
  for he comes to judge the earth.
He will judge the world in righteousness
  and the peoples with equity.

NOTES

A READING FROM PAUL'S LETTER TO THE HEBREWS 1:1-4

¹ In the past God spoke to our ancestors through the prophets at many times and in various ways, ² but in these last days he has spoken to us by his Son, whom he appointed heir of all things, and through whom also he made the universe. ³ The Son is the radiance of God's glory and the exact representation of his being, sustaining all things by his powerful word. After he had provided purification for sins, he sat down at the right hand of the Majesty in heaven. ⁴ So he became as much superior to the angels as the name he has inherited is superior to theirs.

NOTES

A READING FROM THE GOSPEL OF JOHN 1: 1-14 (NIV)

¹ In the beginning was the Word, and the Word was with God, and the Word was God. ² He was with God in the beginning. ³ Through him all things were made; without him nothing was made that has been made. ⁴ In him was life, and that life was the light of all mankind. ⁵ The light shines in the darkness, and the darkness has not overcome it.

⁶ There was a man sent from God whose name was John. ⁷ He came as a witness to testify concerning that light, so that through him all might believe. ⁸ He himself was not the light; he came only as a witness to the light.

⁹ The true light that gives light to everyone was coming into the world. ¹⁰ He was in the world, and though the world was made through him, the world did not recognize him. ¹¹ He came to that which was his own, but his own did not receive him. ¹² Yet to all who did receive him, to those who believed in his name, he gave the right to become children of God— ¹³ children born not of natural descent, nor of human decision or a husband's will, but born of God.

¹⁴ The Word became flesh and made his dwelling among us. We have seen his glory, the glory of the one and only Son, who came from the Father, full of grace and truth.

NOTES

A READING FROM THE GOSPEL OF JOHN 1: 1-14 (MSG)

¹⁻² The Word was first,
  the Word present to God,
  God present to the Word.
The Word was God,
  in readiness for God from day one.
³⁻⁵ Everything was created through him;
  nothing—not one thing!—
  came into being without him.
What came into existence was Life,
  and the Life was Light to live by.
The Life-Light blazed out of the darkness;
  the darkness couldn't put it out.
⁶⁻⁸ There once was a man, his name John, sent by God to point out the way to the Life-Light. He came to show everyone where to look, who to believe in. John was not himself the Light; he was there to show the way to the Light.
⁹⁻¹³ The Life-Light was the real thing:
  Every person entering Life
  he brings into Light.
He was in the world,
  the world was there through him,
  and yet the world didn't even notice.
He came to his own people,
  but they didn't want him.
But whoever did want him,
  who believed he was who he claimed
  and would do what he said,
He made to be their true selves,
  their child-of-God selves.
These are the God-begotten,
  not blood-begotten,
  not flesh-begotten,
  not sex-begotten.

¹⁴ The Word became flesh and blood,
    and moved into the neighborhood.
We saw the glory with our own eyes,
    the one-of-a-kind glory,
    like Father, like Son,
Generous inside and out,
    true from start to finish.

NOTES

CONTEMPLATING *THE GOSPEL OF JOHN*

There is no historical or biblical birthdate for Jesus. After Constantine's requested canon arrived, his mother traveled to identify dates and locations to support the canon. Most often, these dates were appropriated from Pagan celebrations as a means of conversion to Christianity. Christmas and the Winter solstice clearly exemplify this. We can see both reflected in today's reading from the Gospel of John. The words, "The light shines in the darkness, and the darkness has not overcome it" (v 5) easily apply to both celebrations.

Cultures throughout time and around the world celebrate the return of the light. The Roman Winter Solstice celebrated a new solar cycle. Churches subjugate this practice by corresponding Jesus' birth with the return of the sun and by placing the celebration very near the day with the least amount of light. As the story continues, it is part of a spiraling cycle. The church attempts to tell the story as if it is happening for the first time. As a child, I recall memorizing scripture passages and singing hymns to perform in Christmas pageants. Today, I realize this was a way of remembering the story verbatim and a way to instill religious meaning to scriptures. But the story has been told for thousands of years without considering various discoveries, understandings, and conclusions since the canon was established by destroying all other gospels. Set in stone, stories paralyze because they can't adapt to context.

Both the inclusive language translation and the contemporary interpretation of John's version of Jesus' birth retain a focus on God as masculine alone. But the connection to solstice and the sun has always made me think of the moon. The moon connects us to the Divine Feminine and her tides. The solstice always falls near a New Moon, and this year is no different. A variety of planets also typically align at this time. The power of this alignment invites our deepest wishes and desires.

In this light, the following words from *The Gospel of Mary* brought alongside the Gospel of John long after both were written, give the birth of Jesus new meaning:

> **A READING FROM *THE GOSPEL OF MARY*: PAGES 18-19**
>
> "Rather we should be ashamed (atone), clothe ourselves with perfect Humanity (Anthropos), acquire it for ourselves as he instructed us, and preach the gospel, not laying down any other rule or other law beyond what the Savior said.
>
> When Levi said these things, they started to go out and to preach.
>
> The Gospel According to Mary.

Womb Awakening-Year A: Christmas/Solstice

NOTES

CONTEMPLATING *THE GOSPEL OF MARY*

Who can imagine the sun without the moon? The day without the night? Masculine Energy without Feminine Energy? An enlightenment without the teachings of both Jesus and Mary Magdalene?

Without them both, how can we be whole?

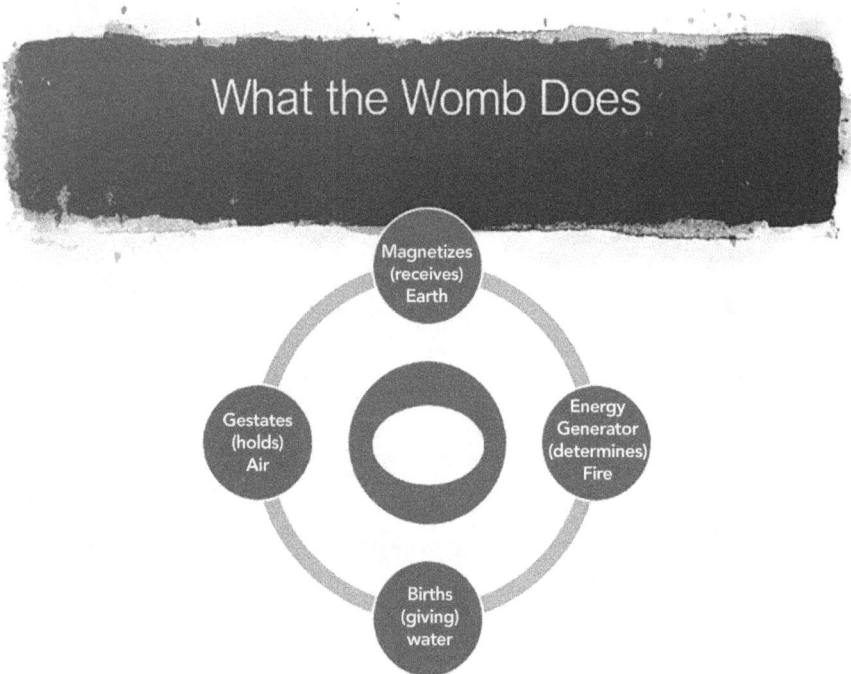

I recently realized this about myself when attending a Womb Awakening Conference coordinated by Kathy Forest. During the live opening, she shared the above elemental womb awakening medicine wheel. While young, our wombs in the Air phase hold. This includes holding any traumas that we may experience. As we develop, our wombs in the Earth phase receive the blood that our bodies use to nurture life that we may either birth or that we may shed and return to the earth in our moon cycles each month.

As we reach the heat of perimenopause, our wombs in the Fire phase generate energy—energy that determines things when we use it consciously. In the Water phase of menopause, we birth energy, wisdom, and light. This is why we celebrate New Moons and Full moons. The rituals are ways to continue our connection to the cycle even when we no longer collect and shed blood. We are so amazingly made that we (including both women and men) can continue to collect and shed energy in a co-creative process.

WHAT IF?

As I listened to Kathy describe each phase, I realized how little I valued my womb and the blood I shed each month. How I limited the value of my womb to reproduction which involved endometriosis, hemorrhaging, surgeries, and waiting to reach menopause so that the bleeding would finally stop. A world with only one energy, either masculine or feminine, can yield nothing but distortions. Patriarchy is a distortion of both the Sacred Masculine seeking dominion and the Divine Feminine being asleep. I was asleep. I objectified my womb energy according to the patriarchy.

What if part of the "Word becoming Flesh," as the gospel of John describes, and the becoming fully human (Anthropos), as *The Gospel of Mary* describes, is about awakening? This is a testament that we always have an option to awaken to both our sovereignty and our co-creative capacities. The truly amazing thing is the advent of harmony that comes when Sacred Masculine and Divine Feminine energies entwine in love—when we become Anthropos. We need both halves of the mystery to develop eyes to see and ears to hear. One, alone, distorts the message as we have witnessed for thousands of years. Let us shine in the darkness!

POST-READING INTEGRATIONS

1. What is your Womb Awakening story? Both men and women have womb-like energy centers that house our creative juices. No womb necessary. The energy is there for men, for menopausal women, for those who have experienced hysterectomies, and everyone in between.

2. Have you ever fallen asleep? If so, recall the circumstances. If not, what could put you to sleep?

3. What does becoming fully human, Anthropos, mean to you?

CHAPTER 10

Initiation–Year A: First Sunday After Christmas/Solstice

PRE-READING REFLECTIONS

1. What experiences have you had with innocent bloodshed?

2. What questions do you have about shedding another's blood?

3. What information do you recall about Jesus in Egypt?

A READING FROM ISAIAH 63: 7-9

7 I will tell of the kindnesses of the Lord,
  the deeds for which he is to be praised,
  according to all the Lord has done for us—
yes, the many good things
  he has done for Israel,
  according to his compassion and many kindnesses.
8 He said, "Surely they are my people,
  children who will be true to me";
  and so he became their Savior.
9 In all their distress he too was distressed,
  and the angel of his presence saved them.[a]
In his love and mercy he redeemed them;
  he lifted them up and carried them

Initiation-Year A: First Sunday After Christmas/Solstice

NOTES

A FIRST TESTAMENT READING FROM PSALM 148

[1] Praise the Lord.[a]
Praise the Lord from the heavens;
   praise him in the heights above.
[2] Praise him, all his angels;
   praise him, all his heavenly hosts.
[3] Praise him, sun and moon;
   praise him, all you shining stars.
[4] Praise him, you highest heavens
   and you waters above the skies.
[5] Let them praise the name of the Lord,
   for at his command they were created,
[6] and he established them for ever and ever—
   he issued a decree that will never pass away.
[7] Praise the Lord from the earth,
   you great sea creatures and all ocean depths,
[8] lightning and hail, snow and clouds,
   stormy winds that do his bidding,
[9] you mountains and all hills,
   fruit trees and all cedars,
[10] wild animals and all cattle,
   small creatures and flying birds,
[11] kings of the earth and all nations,
   you princes and all rulers on earth,
[12] young men and women,
   old men and children.
[13] Let them praise the name of the Lord,
   for his name alone is exalted;
   his splendor is above the earth and the heavens.
[14] And he has raised up for his people a horn,[b]
   the praise of all his faithful servants,
   of Israel, the people close to his heart.

Initiation–Year A: First Sunday After Christmas/Solstice

NOTES

A SECOND TESTAMENT READING FROM PAUL'S LETTER TO THE HEBREWS 2: 10-18

¹⁰ In bringing many sons and daughters to glory, it was fitting that God, for whom and through whom everything exists, should make the pioneer of their salvation perfect through what he suffered. ¹¹ Both the one who makes people holy and those who are made holy are of the same family. So Jesus is not ashamed to call them brothers and sisters.[a] ¹² He says,
"I will declare your name to my brothers and sisters;
 in the assembly I will sing your praises."[b]
¹³ And again,
"I will put my trust in him."[c]
And again he says,
"Here am I, and the children God has given me."[d]

¹⁴ Since the children have flesh and blood, he too shared in their humanity so that by his death he might break the power of him who holds the power of death—that is, the devil— ¹⁵ and free those who all their lives were held in slavery by their fear of death. ¹⁶ For surely it is not angels he helps, but Abraham's descendants. ¹⁷ For this reason he had to be made like them,[e] fully human in every way, in order that he might become a merciful and faithful high priest in service to God, and that he might make atonement for the sins of the people. ¹⁸ Because he himself suffered when he was tempted, he is able to help those who are being tempted.

Initiation–Year A: First Sunday After Christmas/Solstice

NOTES

A READING FROM MATTHEW 2: 13-23 (NIV)

[13] When they had gone, an angel of the Lord appeared to Joseph in a dream. "Get up," he said, "take the child and his mother and escape to Egypt. Stay there until I tell you, for Herod is going to search for the child to kill him."

[14] So he got up, took the child and his mother during the night and left for Egypt, [15] where he stayed until the death of Herod. And so was fulfilled what the Lord had said through the prophet: "Out of Egypt I called my son."[a]

[16] When Herod realized that he had been outwitted by the Magi, he was furious, and he gave orders to kill all the boys in Bethlehem and its vicinity who were two years old and under, in accordance with the time he had learned from the Magi. [17] Then what was said through the prophet Jeremiah was fulfilled:

[18] "A voice is heard in Ramah,
　weeping and great mourning,
Rachel weeping for her children
　and refusing to be comforted,
　because they are no more."[b]

[19] After Herod died, an angel of the Lord appeared in a dream to Joseph in Egypt [20] and said, "Get up, take the child and his mother and go to the land of Israel, for those who were trying to take the child's life are dead."

[21] So he got up, took the child and his mother and went to the land of Israel. [22] But when he heard that Archelaus was reigning in Judea in place of his father Herod, he was afraid to go there. Having been warned in a dream, he withdrew to the district of Galilee, [23] and he went and lived in a town called Nazareth. So was fulfilled what was said through the prophets, that he would be called a Nazarene.

Initiation–Year A: First Sunday After Christmas/Solstice

NOTES

A READING FROM MATTHEW 2: 13-23 (MSG)

¹³ After the scholars were gone, God's angel showed up again in Joseph's dream and commanded, "Get up. Take the child and his mother and flee to Egypt. Stay until further notice. Herod is on the hunt for this child and wants to kill him."
¹⁴⁻¹⁵ Joseph obeyed. He got up, took the child and his mother under cover of darkness. They were out of town and well on their way by daylight. They lived in Egypt until Herod's death. This Egyptian exile fulfilled what Hosea had preached: "I called my son out of Egypt."
¹⁶⁻¹⁸ Herod, when he realized that the scholars had tricked him, flew into a rage. He commanded the murder of every little boy two years old and under who lived in Bethlehem and its surrounding hills. (He determined that age from information he'd gotten from the scholars.) That's when Jeremiah's revelation was fulfilled:
A sound was heard in Ramah,
    weeping and much lament.
Rachel weeping for her children,
    Rachel refusing all solace,
Her children gone,
    dead and buried.
¹⁹⁻²⁰ Later, when Herod died, God's angel appeared in a dream to Joseph in Egypt: "Up, take the child and his mother and return to Israel. All those out to murder the child are dead."
²¹⁻²³ Joseph obeyed. He got up, took the child and his mother, and reentered Israel. When he heard, though, that Archelaus had succeeded his father, Herod, as king in Judea, he was afraid to go there. But then Joseph was directed in a dream to go to the hills of Galilee. On arrival, he settled in the village of Nazareth. This move was a fulfillment of the prophetic words, "He shall be called a Nazarene."

NOTES

CONTEMPLATING *THE GOSPEL OF MATTHEW*

While there is no evidence to support an historical Joseph, or at least the Joseph described in the gospels, there is a suggestion that Joseph is better understood as a legendary figure modeled after the First Testament Joseph, son of Jacob. This Joseph is popularly known as the Joseph with the Coat of Many Colors who was sold into slavery by his brothers. As an Egyptian slave, he found favor with the Pharaoh by interpreting his dreams. He married what researchers refer to as an "impure virgin," Asenath, daughter of Potiphera, priest of On. With her, he had two sons (Genesis 41: 41-51).

The theory makes sense when we note that God speaks to Jesus' father, Joseph, through dreams and that the First Testament Joseph interprets dreams. They both marry women viewed by their cultures as "impure virgins" and have their own children with them. All of the canonical gospels mention Jesus' siblings (Matthew 12: 46-50, Mark 3: 31, Luke 8: 19 and John 2: 12)." I only mention this because some understand a virgin birth to mean that Mary remained a virgin her entire life and never birthed other children. The Gospel of Matthew, itself, leaves the possibility of additional children open with the words in today's reading, "But he did not consummate their marriage until she gave birth to a son. And he gave him the name Jesus" (v 25).

If we consider Joseph modeled after the First Testament Joseph, the "Slaughter of the Innocents" and Joseph's dream instructing him to flee to Egypt to protect his family may remind us of the plague that Moses survived. Jesus is often referred to as The New Moses when described as the Messiah. When Pharaoh changed his mind and refused to free the Israelites, Moses announced that each of the first born would die (Exodus 12:23). This event became the Jewish celebration of Passover. Jesus is passed over by Herod's command to slaughter those born within two years of Jesus' birth.

There is also no historical evidence documenting "The Slaughter of the Innocents" during the time of Jesus' birth estimated at 4-6 BCE. This includes the work of the historian Josephus, most often consulted by biblical scholars. The lack of support furthers the theory of the story metaphorically, modeling Jesus as the new Moses.

The shedding of innocent blood connects the Passover story with the "Slaughter of the Innocents" and the Christian story of Jesus as Paschal lamb, the innocent sacrifice. But just as the sacrifices made in the temples over thousands of years did not end innocent bloodshed, neither did the sacrifice of Jesus. We saw this in the review of The Crusades, the Inquisitions and the Reformation Wars. The lack of results raises questions about shedding any innocent blood.

A READING FROM *THE GOSPEL OF MARY*: PAGE 7

"That's why the Good came among you, up to things of every nature in order to restore it within its root."

Then he continued and said, "That's why you get sick and die, because you love what tricks you. Anyone who can understand should understand!"

Initiation–Year A: First Sunday After Christmas/Solstice

NOTES

CONTEMPLATING *THE GOSPEL OF MARY*

Critics argue that the Gnostic gospels present corrupt human natures. I do not see this in the *The Gospel of Mary*. Instead, I read Jesus' reply to Peter's question about sin, literally stating, "There is no sin," as an indication of our spiritual natures. In today's passage, we read words describing "the Good coming up to things of every nature in order to restore it within its root" documenting that we can become distracted and need to refocus. These works reflect an innate light and shadow in us rather than original sin.

All of us can resonate with our actions taking us away from our nature and roots. When we do not act from our best selves by losing our tempers, plotting with others to benefit at someone's expense, or by not showing up to take responsibility for our lives, we stray from our roots and nature. Doing such things does not mean we are sinful and need a savior. They mean that we have more to learn to realize our full potential.

We can understand the story of the "Slaughter of the Innocents" in this context. In such a case, Herod's decree indicates his straying from his nature and roots. When our egos grow to believe that other lives are expendable if we retain or obtain what we desire, we stray from our nature. If everything is connected, how can any aspect of life be expendable? This includes the gospels excluded from the canon, the Divine Feminine erased from history, the Sacred Masculine compromised as a result, and all life on Earth.

The Egyptian discovery of *The Gospel of Mary*, attributed to Mary Magdalene or a follower, with The Nag Hammadi texts at a minimum, suggests she traveled there as an adult. A variety of scholars suggest that Jesus and Mary Magdalene traveled there together during what is commonly referred to as the "lost years" by Christian scholars. This would mean that Jesus and Mary Magdalene met prior to their meeting described in the gospels. The canonical gospels contain no information about Jesus' whereabouts between the ages of 13 and 29. Given all the confusion about the identity of Mary

Magdalene, it is difficult to identify such a meeting canonically. For me, Mary Magdalene and Mary of Bethany being one and the same person supports the idea of Jesus' meeting Mary Magdalene during the lost years. The gospels do not show their initial meeting, but they do highlight the intimate relationships shared among Jesus, Mary, Martha, and Lazarus.

Others suggest that Jesus traveled elsewhere during these years. Some say that he studied healing in India and returned there when he did not die on the cross but rather escaped. There is even a burial place for Jesus identified in India. Tradition indicates that Joseph of Arimathea was Jesus' great uncle and that he traveled with him along a tin route during the lost years. That route included stops in Egypt, England, and Glastonbury. It is interesting to consider what it would mean if Jesus traveled to these places unaccosted, only to die in Jerusalem when he attempted to apply what he learned.

There are many ways of knowing. In the context of Jesus there is non-religious bible reading, biblical research, religious perspectives of the bible taught in churches, tradition, historical research alone, non-Christian perspectives such as Judaism and its teachings about The First Testament, and the teachings of Islam in the context of the Koran. Adding other ancient Wisdom traditions demonstrates how these perspectives may be sorted out separately or joined in infinite combinations.

WHAT IF?

What if "The Slaughter of the Innocents" is an initiation? Initiations of Jesus and the hearer/reader of the story? This Jesus is not the one of sweet, syrupy hymns such as "Away in a Manger." This Jesus has a target on his back. What if following this Jesus means a target on the follower's back? I wonder if Jesus knew his birth, even if simply a literary device, was associated with innocent bloodshed. If so, how did this impact his life and ministry? Especially when followers sought bloodshed, believing he was the Messiah come to overthrow the Romans?

What a comfort it must have been to meet Mary of Magdala, be she follower and/or consort. She was someone who "got it" and sought to comfort him in the way he came to comfort the world. What if, from the very beginning of his life, we are shown the innocence that will be slaughtered in his name as well as the innocence lost by following his teachings? If so, this story makes clear that innocence is not the goal, but, rather, companionship in suffering is. What if this story is an initiation of wounded healers?

What if we just don't know? What if having eyes to see and ears to hear is about witnessing the actions that remove us from our elemental natures and our roots? We may think we have everything figured out and sorted into sinful and sinless actions. And thinking this, we include and marginalize accordingly, just as the church did with the variety of gospels. Clearly, we lose parts of the story and a way of living. Contemplating a variety of points of view requires patience, listening, and reflection rather than progress at all costs. What if our lives are about standing in the Mystery, unable to know everything at one time, but still needing to choose how we will live each day?

POST-READING INTEGRATIONS

1. What does *The Gospel of Mary* help you understand more clearly?

2. What, if any, initiation have you experienced?

3. What questions arise as we stand in the Mystery, preparing for the next leg of the journey?

Conclusion

POST-READING INTEGRATIONS

1. How would you describe your Spiritual Nature? What part(s) of it have you reclaimed on this Advent, Solstice, Christmas Path?

2. What surprises met you along the way?

3. What do you need for the next leg of the journey?

Conclusion

LIVING IN THE MYSTERY

I live in a magical place where all kinds of birds, a symbol of connection between worlds surround me, Bald Eagles, Falcons, Owls, Hawks, Blue Heron, Cranes, Pelicans, Swans, Orioles, Cardinals, Blue Jays, Nuthatches, Ravens, Crows, Robins, Finches, and Hummingbirds visit. They build nests, lay eggs, raise their young, and migrate for the winter. Through their many travels, they bring lessons for how to live and thrive in the betwixt and between places, the now and not yet moments, of life. Unfortunately, they also lose their eggs to predators, die from disease, fly into windows, and fall to the ground.

A falcon once flew into my studio window and fell dead in our driveway. I especially mourned this loss because Falcon is the spirit animal of my birth. We tried to give his remains to a local tribe for use in ceremony, but our attempts failed. After spending a few days in a box in our garage, we decided to cremate his body in a ceremony celebrating his life. I anointed him with Frankincense and watched an aromatic blue haze rise from the fire. That night, I dreamed that our Goldendoodle, Sarah, and I stood in the backyard of our house. It shined brightly, like the sun shines on fresh snow, but there was no snow. The light was almost blinding. When I could finally look up, I saw a family of white great horned owls in a tree—male, female, and two fledglings. Mom and dad stared at us as the fledglings bobbed back and forth, preparing themselves for eventual flight.

"This is so beautiful," I thought as I awoke. Was the vision a gift from Falcon? Another spirit animal to help guide and affirm my thoughts and actions? An energetic part of the field? I don't have it all figured out yet, but part of the message is that I am held. The image emerges each time I sun gaze in the morning. The birds and other sentient beings join me, announcing the rising of the sun. When we stand together silently as the sun breaks the horizon, this scene assures me that I am loved, or more accurately perhaps, that I *am* love by my connection to the grid of love that sustains life. Then the chirping begins, birds fly away, cocks crow, toads croak, dogs bark, and the sound of traffic begins. As a new day with wonder and promise arises, I realize that I am here to be faithful. Faithful to a journey that is my life garnering wisdom through both light and shadow experiences.

Before I started writing this book, I thought that I left the church by simply resigning from the roster. But, when I finished writing the first draft, I realized a shadow aspect of the process that I needed to address. This is not what I had expected when setting out to accomplish my goal. As my writing mentor, Astara Jane Ashley, asked, "What do we do when our hearts break open in love when we journey inside, and we find no support for our experience?" Many of us self-excommunicate. As I re-read the book to revise it for submission, I realized that the Religious Trauma that I experienced and the Spiritual Bypass that I practiced informed my decision to self-excommunicate by leaving the roster. This made me consider how complicit I was in passing similar experiences on to others while serving in the church.

I found myself wondering: just what is it that I have birthed here? Is it something simply written for myself, for the realizations made in the process of writing? A child that I have labored to deliver that is stillborn? Or have I birthed a new life with clarity of purpose? These questions helped me realize the many ways that religion had not left me just because I left the church roster. Spiritual Bypass allows it to remain within me until I recapitulate all its teachings and the agreements that I made accordingly.

Questions of what to leave behind and what to take with me linger as I am sure they do in many ways for all of us on this Advent/Christmas/Solstice Path. My questions include: Who are Jesus and Mary Magdalene outside of church doctrine and dogma? How may I know them outside of religion? What do I consciously choose to leave behind and choose to take with me as I continue the journey of my life?

Conclusion

Another thing we do when we don't find support around us is to seek it elsewhere. We search for what resonates with our experience(s). Often this leaves us retracing our steps. Colonization and religion separated us from the earth and our spiritual gifts by requiring us to acquiesce to the divine connection of government and church authorities instead of our own. So, we wander purposefully, investigating teachers, reading books, taking trainings, attending programs, and receiving initiations that resonate with our experiences. We realize things about ourselves as we navigate points of choice and reclaim our sovereignty.

While I intended to write a book facilitating a walk within for you, I discovered that the very act of writing it required a walk within for me as well. Is it even possible to help facilitate another's walk within without traveling within oneself? Through a series of recapitulations, not all contained here, I reclaimed my birthright—both Divine Feminine and Sacred Masculine energies. I am learning that I am faithful to no god or goddess, but to the journey. The divine journey of my soul across time, cultures, experiences, words, songs, gestures, and energies emerging within each moment.

Thank you for your companionship on this path and for the contemplative work that you do. It makes a difference to the world. All the agreements that we process in the transition phase of the labor pains, help birth a new Earth. I look forward to traveling through another season with you in the next book of the Unlearning Religious Dogma Series. Until then, I wish you traveling mercies.

Find all the details regarding the next Walk Within *book from the "Unlearning Regious Dogma" series at*
crystalsteinbergcocreating.com

Acknowledgments

We don't know what we don't know. The publishing process underscores the validity of this statement. Every step of the process contains new learnings. I am grateful for the wisdom of my ancestors: Albert, Lulu, Marlene, Tom, Al, Delores, and all whom I have not met in this world, the patience, support, and encouragement of my family: Mike, Chris, Matt, Charleigh, Debbie, Rich, Michael, Diana, Jennifer, Danielle, and friends Robin and Rosie. All of us learned how being accessible to inspired creative flow involves respecting boundaries, sometimes silence, other times active processing, and always awareness of divine presence in everyone.

Many teachers and mentors in a variety of forms enlighten me along the way. To honor them and the gifts they share, I acknowledge them here.

People: Bill Schang, Vance Cope-Kasten, Kathy Babcock, Marc Denning, Nick Hockings, Nathaniel Gillon, Pete Musso, Pat Richter, George Richter, Judith Christopher, Vitor Westhelle, Joy Philip, Moon Sisters, Keith Garafalo, HeatherAsh Amara, and all of my Warrior Goddess Circle Sisters.

Nature Guides: Essential Essences, Plants, Trees, Flowers, Falcon, White Great Horned Owl, Eagle, Swan, Sandhill Crane, Blue Heron, Deer, Coyote, Fox, Bear and Abers, the elements of Earth, Air, Fire, Water and Ether.

Spaces and Land with Consciousness like the Acoma, Hopi, Isleta, Jemez, Nambe', Picuris, Pojoaque, Taos and Zuni Pueblos, the Gathering Space in the LRC and the land stewarded by the Ho-Chunk Nation—Keepers of the Sacred Voice on which we are blessed to live as caretakers.

Books not already mentioned that significantly impact my awareness:

Poetry: by Wendell Barry, Mary Oliver, Kim Blazer, Mark Turcotte, Nikki Giovanni, and Joy Harjo.

Novels/Plays: *The Brothers Karamozov* by Fyodor Dostoevsky, *The Adventures of Huckleberry Finn* by Mark Twain, *Invisible Man* by Ralph Ellison, *Watch for Me on the Mountain* by Forrest Carter, *Silence* by Shusaku Endo, *Song of Solomon* by Toni Morrison, *The Red Tent* by Anita Diamant, and *The Expected One* trilogy by Kathleen McGowan and *The Tempest* by Shakespeare, *Hedda Gabler* by Henrik Ibsen, *The Vagina Monologues* by Eve Ensler, and *Wit* by Margaret Edson.

Philosophy/Theology: Plato, Aristotle, Julian of Norwich, Baruch Spinoza, Soren Kierkegaard, Martin Buber, Paul Tillich, Diana Butler Bass, Marcus Borg, David Rhoads, Elaine Pagels, Phyllis Tribble, and Mirabai Starr.

Indigenous Wisdom: *God is Red* by Vine Deloria Jr., *House Made of Dawn* by Scott Momaday, *Ceremony* by Leslie Marmon Silko, *Lame Deer, Seeker of Visions* by Richard Erdoes, *Lakota Woman* by Mary Crow Dog, *Prison Writings* by Leonard Peltier, *Braiding Sweetgrass* by Robin Wall Kimmerer, and *My Grandmother's Hands* by Resmaa Menakem.

Artwork: by Michelangelo, Leonardo da Vinci, Sofonisba Anguissola, Artemisia Gentileschi, Friedl Dicker-Brandeis and her students in Terezin, Agnes Pelton, Hilma of Klint, Wassily Kandinsky, Paul Klee, Vincent Van Gogh, Claude Monet, Georgia O'Keefe, Frida Kahlo, Fritz Holder, Allan Howser, Malcom Furlow, Kehinde Wiley, and Shara Hughes.

Finally, I especially acknowledge Flower of Life Press and the support staff. They enhance vibration and voices by encouraging authors to write from healing scars rather than open wounds. In this time of Divine Feminine resurgence, the stories we share involve both the suffering in her absence and healing in her presence. Birthing this dual nature requires experienced and wise midwives guiding the process while writers labor and deliver. Within this mystery we not only birth our individual creations, but we also co-create a communal space for vulnerable sharing that grows love. Thank you Astara, Barb, editors, everyone behind the scenes and my Divine Writing Journey sisters. I love you and this book would not exist without you.

Endnotes

1. Adela Suliman and Timothy Bella, "GOP Rep. Boebert: 'I'm tired of this separation of church and state junk,'" *The Washington Post*, June 28, 2022, https://www.washingtonpost.com/politics/2022/06/28/lauren-boebert-church-state-colorado/

2. HeatherAsh Amara, *The Warrior Heart Practice* (New York: St. Martin's Publishing Group, 2020), 20-32.

3. Mark Sameth, "Is God Both Male and Female?" *Forward*, March 13, 2017, https://forward.com/community/365818/is-god-both-male-and-female/

4. Lawrence Schiffman, "Seventy Years of the Dead Sea Scrolls," *The Jerusalem Post*, October 31, 2017, https://www.jpost.com/israel-news/culture/seventy-years-of-the-dead-sea-scrolls-510977

5. Schiffman

6. Shah Zia, "Is the West ready for Islam?" *The Nag Hammadi Library*, February 26, 2010, https://islam4jesus.org/article/the-nag-hammadi-library-1qhnnhcumbuyp-158/

7. Sarah Pulliam Bailey, "Anglican Communion suspends the Episcopal Church after years of gay rights debates," *The Washington Post*, January 14, 2016, https://www.washingtonpost.com/news/acts-of-faith/wp/2016/01/14/anglican-communion-suspends-the-episcopal-church-for-3-years-from-committees/

8. "Where does the Revised Common Lectionary originate?" *The Revised Common Lectionary*, https://lectionary.library.vanderbilt.edu/faq2.php

9. David Wheeler-Reed, "What the early church thought about God's gender," *The Conversation,* August 1, 2018, https://theconversation.com/what-the-early-church-thought-about-gods-gender-100077

10. Gail Cafferata, "Gender, Judicatory Respect and Pastor's Well-Being in Closing Churches," *National Library of Medicine,* May 23, 2020, https://www.ncbi.nlm.nih.gov/pmc/articles/PMC7245186/

11. "Jewish Rites of Purification," Early Church History, https://earlychurchhistory.org/medicine/ancient-jews-cleanliness/

12. "The Great Crusades: A Woman's Role," December 8, 1997, http://websites.umich.edu/~marcons/Crusades/topics/women/women-article.html

13. "The Great Crusades: A Woman's Role"

14. Sharyn Eastaugh, "The Crusade Against the Cathars," History of the Crusades, Episode 113, https://crusadespod.com/assets/Uploads/Episode-113.pdf.

15. "Women of the Reformation," *The Master's University,* https://www.masters.edu/news/women-of-the-reformation.html

16. Joshua Mark, "Ten Women of the Protestant Reformation," *World History Encyclopedia,* March 17, 2022, https://www.worldhistory.org/article/1964/ten-women-of-the-protestant-reformation/

Bibliography

Amara, HeatherAsh. *The Warrior Heart Practice*. New York: St. Martin's Publishing Group, 2020

Cafferata, Gail. "Gender, Judicatory Respect and Pastor's Well-Being in Closing Churches," *National Library of Medicine*. May 23, 2020. https://www.ncbi.nlm.nih.gov/pmc/articles/PMC7245186/

Cherry, Kendra. "What is Spiritual Bypassing?" *Spirituality*. December 6, 2020, https://www.verywellmind.com/spirituality-4157198

Eastaugh, Sharyn. "The Crusade Against the Cathars." History of the Crusades. Episode 113. https://crusadespod.com/assets/Uploads/Episode-113.pdf

Elie, Paul. "Pope Francis's 'Penitential Pilgrimage' to Canada's Indigenous Communities," *The New Yorker*, July 26, 2022, https://www.newyorker.com/news/daily-comment/pope-franciss-penitential-pilgrimage-to-canadas-indigenous-communities

Forest, Kathy. Great Womb Awakening Conference. June 20, 2022. https://www.greatwombawakening-2/event-schedule.com

Funk, Betsy and Topaz Weis. Class Notes from "Exploring and Mourning Ancestral Roots as Spiritual Practice." Creativity and Expressive Therapies Summit. New York: November 7, 2021.

Garrison, Jim, Curator. Humanity Rising Days 1-10, *Elder Presentations*. Ubiquity University, beginning May 22, 2020. https://www.youtube.com/watch?v=N85YLWc5N7U&t=10s

Heart Math Institute. https://www.heartmath.org

Hummel, Charles E. "The Faith Behind the Famous: Isaac Newton." *Christianity Today*. July/August 2022

"Jewish Rites of Purification." *Early Church History.* https://earlychurchhistory.org/medicine/ancient-jews-cleanliness/

Locher, John. "The Pope's Apology to Indigenous People Doesn't Go Far Enough, Canada Says." The Associated Press, July 28, 2022. https://www.npr.org/2022/07/28/1114207125/canada-pope-apology-indigenous

Mark, Joshua. "Ten Women of the Protestant Reformation." *World History Encyclopedia.* March 17, 2022. https://www.worldhistory.org/article/1964/ten-women-of-the-protestant-reformation/

Mattison, Mark. "*The Gospel of Mary* Translation." https://www.gospels.net/mary

McGilchrist, Iain. *The Master and His Emissary.* Connecticut: Yale University Press, 2019

Osorio, Carlos. "Pope Calls Treatment of Indigenous in Canada Schools 'Genocide'". *The New York Times,* July 30, 2022. https://www.aljazeera.com/news/2022/7/30/pope-calls-treatment-of-indigenous-in-canada-schools-genocide

Pulliam Bailey, Sarah. "Anglican Communion suspends the Episcopal Church after years of gay rights debates." *The Washington Post.* January 14, 2016. https://www.washingtonpost.com/news/acts-of-faith/wp/2016/01/14/anglican-communion-suspends-the-episcopal-church-for-3-years-from-committees/

Sameth, Mark. "Is God Both Male and Female?" *Forward.* March 13, 2017. https://forward.com/community/365818/is-god-both-male-and-female/

Schiffman, Lawrence. "Seventy Years of the Dead Sea Scrolls." *The Jerusalem Post.* October 31, 2017. https://www.jpost.com/israel-news/culture/seventy-years-of-the-dead-sea-scrolls-510977

Shah Zia. "Is the West ready for Islam?" *The Nag Hammadi Library.* February 26, 2010. https://islam4jesus.org/article/the-nag-hammadi-library-1qhnnhcumbuyp-158/

Stuart. "The Destruction of Non-Canonical Texts." Biblical Criticism and History Forum. May 21, 2020, https://earlywritings.com/forum/viewtopic.php?t=7018

Suliman, Adela and Timothy Bella. "GOP Rep. Boebert: 'I'm tired of this separation of church and state junk.'" *The Washington Post.* June 28, 2022. https://www.washingtonpost.com/politics/2022/06/28/lauren-boebert-church-state-colorado/

"The Great Crusades: A Woman's Role." December 8, 1997. http://websites.umich.edu/~marcons/Crusades/topics/women/women-article.html

Walker, Barbara. "80-90 million Wise Women were murdered during Inquisition . . . Suppression of the mother." Freethought Today. https://steemit.com/life/@quantummonks/80-90-million-wise-women-were-murdered-during-inquisition-suppression-of-the-mother

Wheeler-Reed, David. "What the early church thought about God's gender." *The Conversation.* August 1, 2018. https://theconversation.com/what-the-early-church-thought-about-gods-gender-100077

"Where does the Revised Common Lectionary Originate?" The Revised Common Lectionary Library. https://lectionary.library.vanderbilt.edu/faq2.php

"Women of the Reformation." The Masters University. https://www.masters.edu/news/women-of-the-reformation.html

About the Author

As the creator of the Unlearning Religious Dogma Series, **Crystal Steinberg** writes for anyone exploring their spiritual nature. Sharing experiences from her personal journey, she inspires readers to identify their knowings (agreements) and how they acquire them.

Her MAT, MDiv, Certifications and Wisdom Studies PhD Candidate credentials demonstrate research scholarship, while her teaching, ordination, parish service, intuitive healing, initiations, and intentional co-creativity reveal her willingness to serve.

Crystal synthesizes material and spiritual worlds, masculine and feminine energies, and ancient and future understandings to bring Wholeness forward in the chaos of birthing a new world. This Wholeness offers Compassion, Love and Beauty.

Crystal writes in her scriptorium, makes custom nesting dolls in her studio, and speaks and facilitates workshops virtually or locally in nature's magical lake environment of central Wisconsin.

Learn about all of her offerings at **crystalsteinbergcocreating.com**.

More Books by Flower of Life Press

floweroflifepress.com

www.ingramcontent.com/pod-product-compliance
Lightning Source LLC
Chambersburg PA
CBHW071708160426
43195CB00012B/1622